Chicago
RUNNING
Guide

CITY RUNNING GUIDE SERIES

BRENDA BARRERA
with ELIOT WINEBERG

Human Kinetics

Library of Congress Cataloging-in-Publication Data

Barrera, Brenda, 1962-
    Chicago running guide / Brenda Barrera, Eliot Wineberg.
        p.   cm. -- (City running guide series)
    ISBN 0-7360-0132-8
        1. Running--Illinois--Chicago--Guidebooks.   2. Chicago (Ill.)--Guidebooks.   I.
    Wineberg, Eliot, 1964-   II. Title.   III. Series.
    GV1061.22.I3   B37   2000
    917.73'110443--dc21   99-056797

ISBN: 0-7360-0132-8

Acquisitions Editor: Martin Barnard; **Managing Editor**: Leigh LaHood; **Copyeditor**: Lisa Morgan; **Proofreader**: Julie A. Marx; **Graphic Designers**: Stuart Cartwright and Nancy Rasmus; **Graphic Artist**: Sandra Meier; **Cover Designer**: Jack W. Davis; **Photographer (cover and interior)**: Tom Roberts; **Illustrator:** Argosy; **Printer**: Versa Press

On the cover: The lakefront path, featuring the skyline of downtown Chicago, is just one of many terrific routes in and around the city.

Human Kinetics books are available at special discounts for bulk purchase. Special editions or book excerpts can also be created to specification. For details, contact the Special Sales Manager at Human Kinetics.

Printed in the United States of America   10   9   8   7   6   5   4   3   2   1

Human Kinetics
Web site: http://www.humankinetics.com/

United States: Human Kinetics
P.O. Box 5076
Champaign, IL 61825-5076
1-800-747-4457
e-mail: humank@hkusa.com

Canada: Human Kinetics
475 Devonshire Road Unit 100
Windsor, ON N8Y 2L5
1-800-465-7301 (in Canada only)
e-mail: humank@hkcanada.com

Europe: Human Kinetics
P.O. Box IW14
Leeds LS16 6TR, United Kingdom
+44 (0)113-278 1708
e-mail: humank@hkeurope.com

Australia: Human Kinetics
57A Price Avenue
Lower Mitcham, South Australia 5062
(08) 82771555
e-mail: liahka@senet.com.au

New Zealand: Human Kinetics
P.O. Box 105-231
Auckland Central
09-523-3462
e-mail: humank@hknewz.com

CONTENTS

INTRODUCTION

There's a reason Chicago offers the best urban running in the country, and it dates back to 1909, when Daniel Burnham and his assistant, Edward Bennett, created the Plan for Chicago. This city planning landmark called for our shoreline to remain publicly owned, with plenty of beaches and recreational space, thus making it possible to have an 18-mile lakefront path free of cars and situated with an abundance of regular turf for thousands of runners. The Plan for Chicago also called for the development of an extensive park system. With more than 7,400 acres of green space, there's always a neighborhood park to run in wherever you are in the city. Also, the plan defined a systematic arrangement of streets and avenues. Instead of rotundas and winding narrow cobblestone streets, we have a pretty straightforward grid and numbering system that makes it easy to figure your mileage. State St. is the north-south baseline, and Madison St. the east-west baseline. The street numbers increase by 100s per block, and each block is an eighth of a mile, so eight blocks equal one mile. And in addition to the many possible routes in the city, the abundant forest preserves in Cook County and the outlying counties provide a plethora of running options!

Like most runners, I plead guilty to limiting my training runs to the closest, most convenient location (for me, the lakefront path). I hope you will open yourself to new venues. This past year has been a journey in which I discovered trails and courses I never imagined would be so inspiring. My knowledge of the suburbs has increased twofold, and it's been great fun to join the area running clubs whose members I get to catch a glimpse of at races. I've run some hills where I'm sure the locals are still chuckling about my response as I was gasping for air, "Oh, my gosh! This is really tough!" Some trails had few runners, which was a bit unnerving because I'm used to always having people within sight. Exploring those trails brought to light new safety concerns and a confirmation that the buddy system is always important. Even if you're a seasoned runner, I hope you'll take a few minutes to review the safety section.

Because Chicago has so many neighborhood parks and forest preserves, this guide could have been twice as thick as it is. So think of it as a starting block. In deciding which courses to include, I contacted most of the area running clubs, consulted local experts, and polled runners for their suggestions. One of the best ways to discover a new venue is to join a local club on their regular run; I can assure you, they're all very friendly. Most of the forest preserves are well maintained and have excellent maps and outdoor facilities. Other criteria I used to evaluate locations: Is this a popular spot with runners? Is it easy to shorten or lengthen the route? Does it connect to other trails? Is there a variety of easy and tough courses? Will this course appeal to seasoned as well as beginning runners? My hope is that you will use this guide as an opportunity to put some spark into your training regimen and enjoy some routes you've never run before.

Be sure to check with a medical professional before starting a running program if you've never exercised before or are over 40 years old. Build your mileage gradually; never increase more than 10 percent per week. A lot of the trails are one-way; it's okay to go part way and build up to the increased mileage.

TRANSPORTATION

Getting around Chicago is pretty darn easy if you familiarize yourself with the public transportation system. For $1.50 you can get a CTA pass and take the "el" train (the lines are color-coded for easy identification) or a bus (identified by number and destination stop or street name). Most CTA stations have excellent maps and schedule information to help you navigate the city. Metra stations can take you to many suburban locations. Metra trains are the suburban counterpart to the "el" and serve Cook, DuPage, Lake, Will, McHenry, and Kane counties. Ticket prices vary depending on destination, but a good deal is a $5 weekend pass.

There's no question that driving in Chicago can be a pain. Delays are inevitable, especially during rush hours (6–9 A.M. and 3–7 P.M. Monday–Friday). Many of the expressways are referred to by names rather than numbers. Here's a quick reference:

- Dan Ryan Expressway = I-90/I-94 from I-290 south
- Kennedy Expressway = I-90/I-94 to the junction and then I-90 until it becomes the Northwest Tollway

- Edens Expressway = I-94 north of the junction with the Kennedy
- Eisenhower Expressway = I-290
- East-West Tollway = I-88
- North-South Tollway = I-355
- Stevenson Expressway = I-55
- Tri-State Tollway = I-294 and then I-94 north of Lake Rd.

With 1.3 million cars registered in Chicago, trying to find parking can cut into your run time and raise your blood pressure. Many neighborhoods, especially on the near North Side, have restricted parking. The lakefront does offer several parking options, and if you are out early in the morning you can usually find parking on side streets, but check the signs to see if it's restricted. If you're heading downtown, the best bet is going to be a parking garage (or a side street if it's early in the morning on a weekend). And don't forget about cabs ($1.60 to start and $1.40 each mile). I'll admit that on long runs I usually carry money for a cab in case the view of the skyline is just too glorious or I hook up with longwinded friends and end up going further than I'd planned. Finally, many urban dwellers don't own cars, so here's an idea: why not rent a car for the weekend and divide the cost with your carless buddies? I've often used Rent-A-Wreck, and the cost is reasonable.

WEATHER

Hate to break the news, but even though Chicago is nicknamed "The Windy City," and we do experience blustery conditions and cool breezes flowing off the lake, it is not the windiest city in the United States. In 1893, a reporter covering the World Columbian Exposition noted that we Chicagoans couldn't stop bragging about our town— hence the nickname. Our windspeed average is only 10.4 m.p.h., but we still like to brag!

Temperature averages are 21 degrees Fahrenheit in January, 73 degrees in July, and 53 degrees in October. You can expect extreme conditions in any season, from summer heat advisories with ozone alerts to winter snowstorms. The lake effect makes the city warmer than the suburbs in the winter and cooler in the summer.

For summer running, work out early in the morning or later in the afternoon when the temperatures are lower. Drink plenty of fluids, wear light-colored clothing, and run at a slower pace or shorten the distance. Finally, take advantage of the lake water and cool yourself off if your course is along the lakefront.

Winter running can take its toll. Storms have closed down Lake Shore Dr., but the Chicago Park District is pretty good about keeping the lakefront path plowed. Chicagoans are not too proud to wear appropriate attire. Some winter tips: dress in layers, wear thermal gear, and pick out a fun, warm hat. The best advice for winter running is to follow the weather reports and listen to the direction of the wind. In the winter, you always want to run against the wind going out and have it on your back going home. Almost all of the public water fountains and restrooms are closed during the winter months.

Springtime in Chicago is sandwiched between winter gloom and an overnight emerald landscape, where the weather can run the gamut from snow, hail, and rain to temperatures of 70 degrees. By the same token, fall conditions can include wet snow and bone chilling showers. Surface conditions can be deceiving from slick ice to muddy trails, so use caution to avoid injury. The pleasures of running in the springtime or fall are heightened by viewing the transformation of grays to budding pastels and greens to golden-red brilliance.

SAFETY

Let's start with the lakefront. During the summer this path can be as congested as the Dan Ryan Expressway, with a dangerous combination of runners, walkers, bikers, and in-line skaters vying for the same space. My best advice: run as you drive—defensively—and pay attention to avoid any collisions. Look behind you when you cross the path; if you're with a group, try not to have more than two abreast; keep to the far right; if you need to pass someone, make sure there's plenty of room; and if you need to stop, pull over to the side—off the path. If your training partner is your dog, the law requires pets to be leashed.

Some areas of the city are more heavily populated than others, so you might feel more secure in those areas. But keep in mind that crime can happen anywhere and to anyone in the city *and* in the suburbs. The Road Runners Club of America has developed an excellent set of safety guidelines for women runners that can apply to men as well. The guidelines have been slightly modified for this book. You may not follow all of them, but they form a solid set of "rules of the road," whether you're on your home turf or exploring some new trails.

1. Don't wear a headset. Use your ears to be aware of your surroundings.
2. Carry coins for a phone call.

3. Run with a partner.

4. Write down or leave word of the direction of your run. Friends and family should know the particulars of your favorite running routes.

5. If you're running in an unfamiliar area, check out in advance where the phones are and be alert to the location of stores and businesses that will be open. In familiar areas, alter your running pattern occasionally.

6. Always stay alert. Don't run or exceed your capacity when excessively tired.

7. Whenever possible, avoid unpopulated areas, deserted streets, and overgrown trails. Avoid unlit areas at night, and when possible, run clear of bushes or parked cars.

8. Carry ID—name, phone number, blood type, and any appropriate medical information. Avoid wearing conspicuous jewelry.

9. Ignore verbal harassment and use discretion in acknowledging strangers. Look directly at others and be observant, but keep your distance and keep moving.

10. When possible (and when it's safe to do so), run against traffic so you can observe approaching automobiles.

11. Be especially cautious about running in twilight or before dawn, and wear reflective material.

12. Use your intuition about a person or an area. React according to your intuition and avoid either if you're unsure.

13. Carry a whistle or noisemaker.

14. If possible, memorize license tags or identifying characteristics of suspicious cars or strangers.

15. Call police immediately if something happens to you or someone else or you notice anyone behaving suspiciously.

ICON KEY

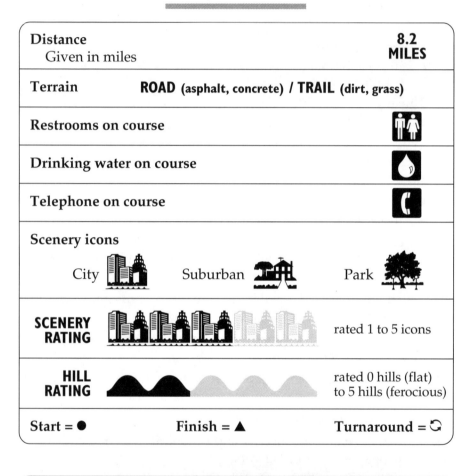

Distance Given in miles	**8.2** **MILES**
Terrain	**ROAD** (asphalt, concrete) / **TRAIL** (dirt, grass)
Restrooms on course	👫
Drinking water on course	💧
Telephone on course	☎
Scenery icons	City 🏙 Suburban 🏘 Park 🌳
SCENERY RATING	rated 1 to 5 icons
HILL RATING	rated 0 hills (flat) to 5 hills (ferocious)
Start = ●	Finish = ▲ Turnaround = ↻

1.8 MILES	ROAD/TRAIL 👫 💧 ☎	SCENERY RATING	🌳🌳🌳🌳
		HILL RATING	

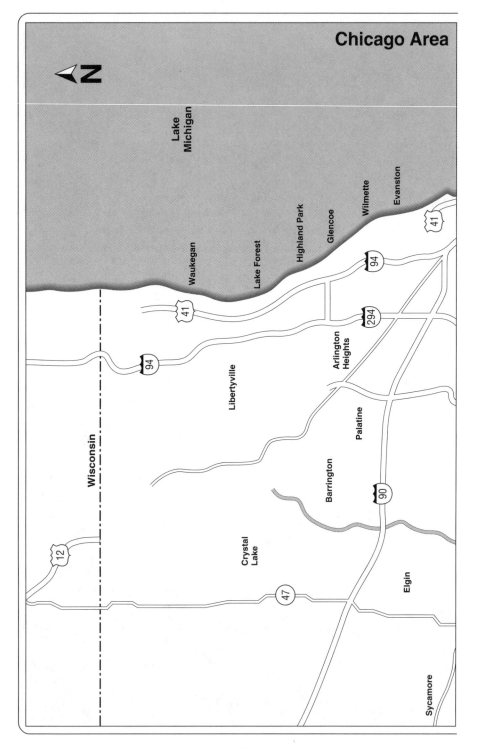

Chicago Area

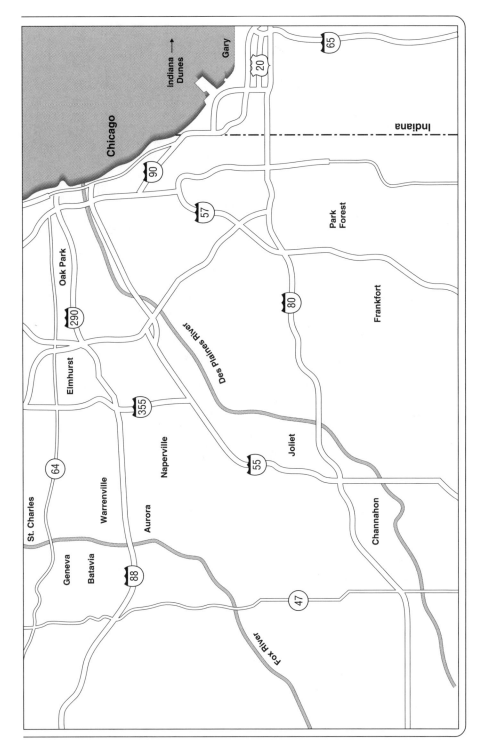

THE CITY

The lakefront is common ground, a ribbon of green that beckons to a rainbow of humanity—black, white, red, yellow, and brown.

—Chicago Tribune architecture critic Blair Kamin,
1999 Pulitzer Prize for Criticism

1. Chicago Lakefront North (Hollywood Beach to Diversey Harbor)
2. Chicago Lakefront Central (Diversey Harbor to Grant Park)
3. Chicago Lakefront South (Grant Park to South Shore Cultural Center)
4. Hyde Park
5. Indian Boundary Trail North
6. Magnificent Mile
7. North Side Landmarks Run

Chicago's lakefront reflects the diversity among our population—rich and varied and an exciting blend of different cultures and languages. This is the most popular and recommended spot for runners thanks to the uninterrupted paths, shimmering waterfront, and skyline filled with architectural masterpieces. The lakefront path stretches from the far north end at Hollywood Beach through Lincoln Park (the largest metropolitan park in the United States) to the historical South Shore Cultural Center. It's reassuring to know the Chicago Police Department's Bicycle Patrol Unit can be seen on all areas of the lakefront from mid-April to mid-October, but be sure to adhere to the safety precautions listed in the introduction (pages viii-ix).

1

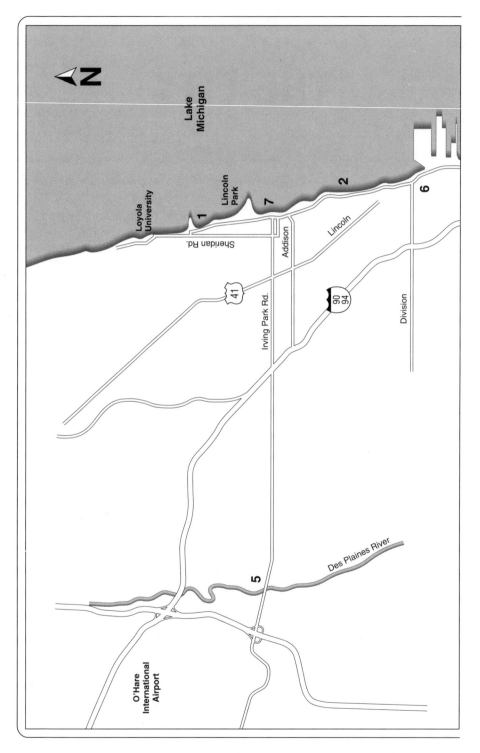

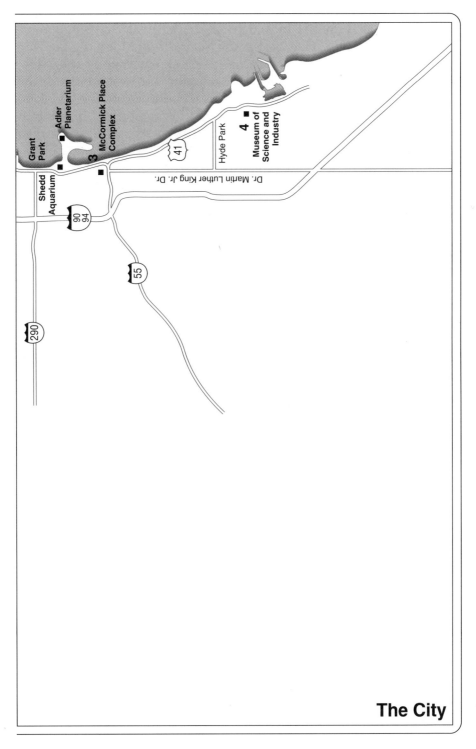

The City

A recent survey found Chicago the most often visited city for domestic business travelers. Here's a tip: the Magnificent Mile is a great way to access the lakefront path and scope out your entertainment agenda, as you'll pass by some of the best shopping and restaurants in the country. A little homesick for plush forest and trail running? Look no further than the Indian Boundary Trail (for safety and better trail conditions, we've included only the northern section). I encourage everyone to be a little adventurous, hop off the beaten cinder path, and explore Chicago's famous neighborhoods. The North Side Landmarks Run will guide you through Wrigleyville and the Lakeview and Ravenswood neighborhoods. Discover (or rediscover) our famous ivy-covered ballpark (hello baseball fans!) and the final resting spots of some of Chicago's titans (I did say this was adventurous). Not too far west of here is a street worth mentioning: Western Ave., at 24.5 miles, is the world's longest continuous street within city limits. The Hyde Park run is equally impressive; try this route once and you'll understand why *plaisance* means "place of pleasure"—and you'll surely want to return to explore the various loops through both Washington and Jackson parks.

A prime time to run in the city is early on the weekend, when you can savor the solitude and, for a few moments—however brief—feel like you've got this whole magnificent playground to yourself. Enjoy!

CHICAGO LAKEFRONT NORTH (HOLLYWOOD BEACH TO DIVERSEY HARBOR)

4.5 MILES	ROAD/TRAIL [icons]	SCENERY RATING [buildings rating]
		HILL RATING [hills rating]

What makes Chicago one of the best running cities in the country? The 18-mile path that borders our best natural asset, Lake Michigan, is so convenient, you can just lace up your shoes and be ready to explore. The path's half-mile markers make it easy to keep track of your mileage.

ACCESS

Hollywood Beach trailhead: By car, take Lake Shore Dr. to Hollywood, where there is limited on-street parking. Parking lots are available at Montrose or Foster Beach, which are a bit south of the path's start by the lakeshore. By CTA, take the Red line to Bryn Mawr. By bus, #145 will take you to Wilson St., #146 to Berwyn St., or #151 to Sheridan Rd./Lake Shore Dr., then go east to the path by the lakeshore. For more information, call the CTA/RTA at 312-836-7000, or visit their Web site at **http://www.transitchicago.com**.

Diversey Harbor (CARA Board) trailhead: By car, take Lake Shore Dr. and exit on Belmont, then head south on Lake Shore Dr. West to Diversey Pkwy. Or exit on Fullerton Pkwy. and head north on Cannon Dr. (the path is right by the road); there is a parking lot on Diversey Pkwy. and limited parking on streets or lots in the area.

By CTA, take the Red line to Fullerton or Belmont, then the Brown line to Diversey. (Note: The train does not run south of Belmont on Sundays.) By bus, take the #74 Fullerton, #76 Diversey; #146, #145, or #151 Sheridan/Lake Shore Dr.; #36 or #22 Clark St. and Broadway.

COURSE

Officially, this route starts at Ardmore St. (5800 N) and Hollywood Beach, but the green trail 0-mile marker is a half mile south at Bryn Mawr Ave.

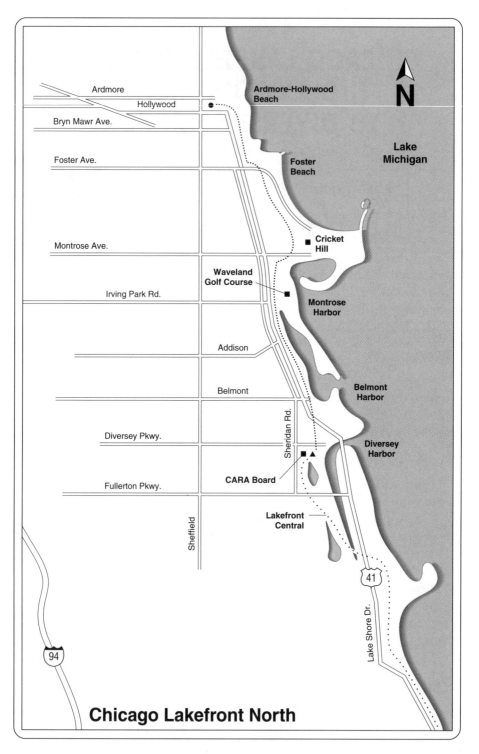

Chicago Lakefront North

More than likely you'll run this section backward, starting at the Chicago Area Runners Association (CARA) Board, and head north.

This flat asphalt-and-cinder path will take you past some memorable points. The first is the Foster Ave. Beach House and basketball court (during high winds the waves are spectacular). The path forks and you can either follow the running path (to the left) or the paved bike path next to Lake Shore Dr. Cricket Hill is our token urban hill and a popular spot, especially for cross country runners. Follow the path by the seawall next to the Sydney Marovitz Golf Course, also known as Waveland Golf Course (312-245-0909), with its historic clock tower (water and restroom available). This seawall section floods in the springtime and can be very icy throughout winter months. From here you'll run into a wooded stretch by the fenced bird sanctuary and emerge near Addison St. and a well-known landmark: the wooden totem pole, Kwansila (means *thunderbird*). This is a popular turnaround spot and meeting place for clubs like the Frontrunners/Frontwalkers. From here to Belmont the running and bike paths join and you'll hear playful barking from the "dog beach" before Belmont Harbor. Please use caution; this is an extremely congested area prone to bicycle/pedestrian accidents. The running path goes to the right under the equestrian trail overpass to a tree-lined stretch next to the driving range. Just a few steps beyond the parking lot is the CARA Board, where the Lincoln Park Pacers and various training groups convene. Be sure to check here for up-to-date information on local races. Restrooms and water are by the entrance to the driving range and are open during warm weather. For wintertime emergencies, runners have often used nearby restaurants or hospitals. Just a few feet from the 4.5-mile marker is the water trough, where you can find running water year round.

Additional courses: At the north edge of Waveland Golf Course, add a 1.7-mile out-and-back run along the edge by the boats and harbor and then the outer path by the lakefront of Montrose Harbor. Scenic spots include Royko's Grove in the southwest corner, a memorial to the Pulitzer Prize-winning *Chicago Tribune* columnist, Mike Royko, who admired this view of the city. Also worth your time is a jaunt through the "Magic Hedge" at Montrose Point, a splendid haven and birding hotspot.

TIP

Breakfast at the Waveland Cafe, next to the clock tower, is a great way to start your weekend after a long run, but it's only open from mid-March through mid-October.

CHICAGO LAKEFRONT CENTRAL (DIVERSEY HARBOR TO GRANT PARK)

5.5 MILES	ROAD/TRAIL	SCENERY RATING	
		HILL RATING	

Shakespeare said, "All the world's a stage." When you reach the Shedd Aquarium, stop along the seawall steps leading to Adler Planetarium and turn your gaze upon Chicago's stage. Like the Globe Theatre, Chicago rose from the ashes and today displays a whole cast of architectural styles rising behind a curtain of cool blue water. It's breathtaking; see if you agree.

ACCESS

Diversey Harbor (CARA Board) trailhead: See Chicago Lakefront North.

  Grant Park trailhead: By car, from the north take Lake Shore Dr. to Museum Campus/Roosevelt Rd. Turn right, then left to Columbus Dr. to McFetridge Dr. From the south, turn at signs for Museum Campus/ McFetridge Dr. Take I-290 directly into the Loop or I-90/I-94; follow signs for "Chicago Loop," which include several access streets. Parking lots are located south of Shedd Aquarium at Soldier Field, and off Solidarity Dr. there is metered parking. By CTA, take the Red, Green, or Orange lines to Harrison or Roosevelt, go east to Lake Shore Dr. By bus, take the #146 Marine/Michigan or #6 Jeffery Express.

COURSE

Right by the 4.5-mile marker, across from North Pond, you'll find the most popular drinking venue for runners—the water trough—with running water year round. Continue past the Lincoln Park Zoo. It's free, so you might want to make a detour to say hello to the animals. In the wintertime, this stretch is pretty dark, but the zoo's holiday decorations provide colorful lighting. You'll pass the Ulysses S. Grant statue and

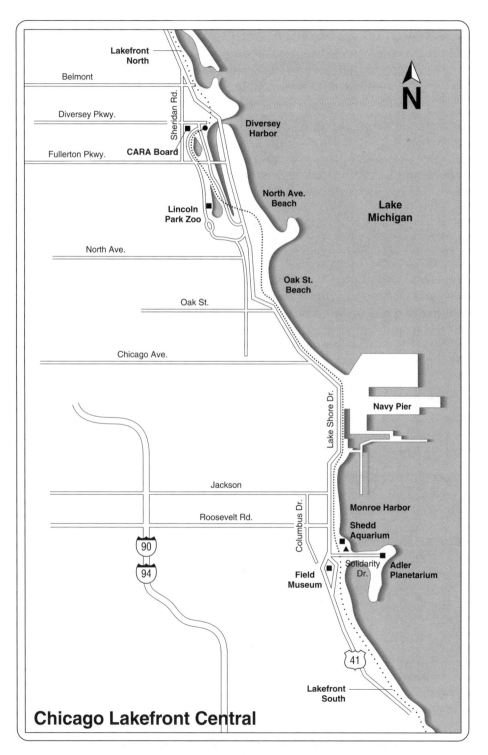

Chicago Lakefront Central

cross the road to the North Ave. bridge to the lakefront paved path. Note: this is a bicycle/pedestrian alert zone; stay to your right.

The first highlight as you head south is the nautical-shaped North Ave. Beach House and immediately beyond, the Chess Pavilion. This is one of my favorite views of the city—take in the John Hancock Center and the 150-foot-high Ferris wheel at Navy Pier. If you run down by the water's edge along the cement strip, stay close to the edge to avoid the sloped pavement. Continue to Oak St. Beach, where distractions include jugglers and bathing beauties. Ohio St. Beach is a good turn-around spot. Take off your training shoes and walk into the cool (ahem, cold) water, a perfect recovery method for sore legs. The path winds by Navy Pier, then over the Chicago River, and you'll pass the Chicago Yacht Club and Monroe Harbor, with the grand architecture of Chicago looming over your shoulder. Options include running on the upper level by Lake Shore Dr. or lower sidewalk by the harbor. You've now entered Museum Campus, with the neoclassical Field Museum ahead. Follow the path around Shedd Aquarium and up to Burnham Harbor at the 10-mile marker.

Additional courses: North Pond loop: .8 mile; North Ave. bridge/ Fieldhouse loop: .5 mile; CARA Board/Diversey Harbor loop: 1.2 miles.

FOOT NOTES

Navy Pier is a favorite Chicago tourist attraction and landmark. Activities include the Chicago Children's Museum and the IMAX Theatre. For information, call 312-595-PIER.

HECKLER SAILS PAST THE COMPETITION

In 1998 Vic Heckler ran a 4:50:22 mile to set pending national and world records—in the 55-59 age group! He also set a U.S. 3,000-meter indoor record (9:33:25) and 5K record (16:07) in 1997. Where does he train? "My first preference is always to run on the lakefront path," Heckler said. Just past the Diversey Harbor parking lot exit by Fullerton Ave., he's marked out a spot starting at the first tree for 300-meter repeats. "I like this because it's a nice wide, straight area," he said. This also gives him another excuse to stay in touch with his second passion, sailing. The CARA Board/Diversey Harbor loop not only adds some mileage but an opportunity to check on his boat, docked in the harbor. The lakefront path is certainly a social venue, and Heckler admits that on any given day he can hook up with some fast talent without making advance plans.

CHICAGO LAKEFRONT SOUTH (GRANT PARK TO SOUTH SHORE CULTURAL CENTER)

7.5 MILES	TRAIL	SCENERY RATING	
		HILL RATING	

CARA Marathon Training Program coordinator Bill Fitzgerald recommends this run for the serenity and has dubbed this the "Ohh and Ahh" section of the Chicago lakefront. Indeed, you will probably utter these exclamations more than once.

ACCESS

Grant Park trailhead: See Chicago Lakefront Central.

South Shore Cultural Center trailhead: By car, take Lake Shore Dr. south to S. South Shore Dr. and E. 71st St., or follow Hyde Park information, page 14. By Metra, take the Chicago Electric-South Chicago Branch to South Shore. By bus, take the #6 Jeffery Express from State St. to 63rd/ Stony Island and #27. For more information, call the CTA/RTA at 773-836-7000, or visit their Web site at **http://www.metrarail.com**.

COURSE

Start at the 10-mile marker at Solidarity Dr. The path snakes through Burnham Harbor, where you can't miss the classical pillars of Soldier Field—home of "da Bears," the Chicago Fire, and large-scale rock concerts. You'll pass by Chicago's oldest statue, Balbo Monument. This is followed by "convention central," McCormick Place, where you'll hear and maybe feel the spray from the outdoor waterfall cascading down from Level 3. A short distance from the shore, if you think you see a propeller plane, you're correct. Since 1948, Northerly Island has been home to Meigs Field Airport. From here, with the exception of the 31st St. Beach House and a few playgrounds and basketball courts, you are treated to uninterrupted lakeshore vistas, wide grass fields, and

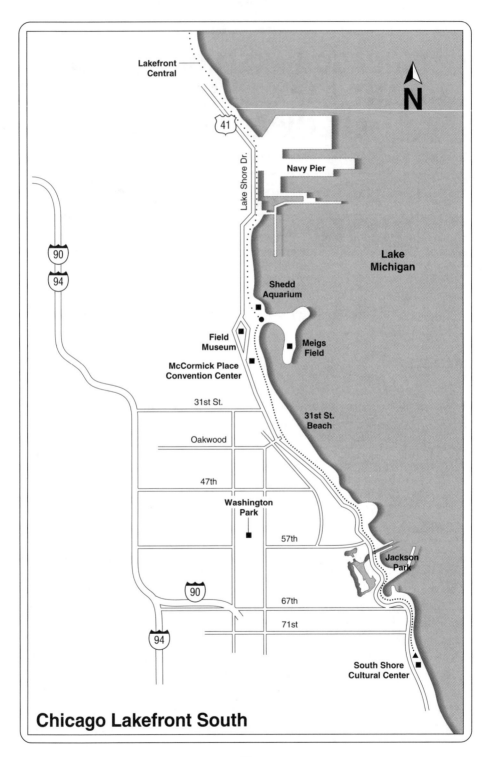

Chicago Lakefront South

surprising inclines before you reach Hyde Park's Promontory Point and the Museum of Science and Industry. Since 1979, this has been home turf for the Rainbow Road Runners Club. They meet at the Promontory Point water fountain the first Sunday of each month at 8 A.M.

The final two miles feature noteworthy South Side landmarks that merit the extra effort: Jackson Park Yacht Club and Pavilion, and at the tail end, South Shore Cultural Center. During most hours this is a noisy section, with Lake Shore Dr. a few feet away, but one of my favorite spots is the wooden footbridge at Marquette Dr.—the concrete bridge next to it has some cool gargoyles. If you're goal-oriented, it's very gratifying to see the 0-mile marker by 71st. St.

Safety notice: even though the mountain-bike police patrol the lakefront path regularly during summer months, this is the least-populated section; recommended running time is early morning, and never run alone.

Additional courses: What better place to greet the rising sun than Adler Planetarium? To add .8 mile, take Solidarity Dr. and circle the planetarium, noting "America's Courtyard," a Stonehenge-inspired sculpture of 60 stones positioned to replicate the galaxy. There's a terrific view of the horizon, and then you get to the north side and see the glorious skyline—"Ohh!" The Promontory Point loop, at .4 mile, includes the David Wallach Fountain with fawn on top (where you can take the underpass to Hyde Park; see page 14), and around this peninsula of jagged rocks you can see another stunning view of the horizon and skyline—"Ahh!"

FOOT NOTES

The South Shore Cultural Center makes a great destination run. Formerly a private country club, now run by the Chicago Park District, it's listed on the National Register of Historic Places. Activities include jazz and gospel concerts, a public nine-hole golf course, theater, and many classes for young and old. For more information, call 312-747-2536.

HYDE PARK

5.1- MILE LOOP	ROAD	SCENERY RATING	
	🚻 💧 ☎	HILL RATING	

This South Side historic jaunt is just steps from the lakefront. It's a great flat course if you want to add mileage to a long run or tour the focal point of Chicago liberalism—the prestigious University of Chicago. Here's a quick trivia question: What 1989 movie, directed by Rob Reiner and involving the zany romance between two U of C graduates, was filmed on campus? See answer on page 16.

ACCESS

Just a 15-minute trip from downtown. By car, the best way is via Lake Shore Dr.; exit at 57th St. Metered parking is plentiful, plus there are spots near the 55th St. underpass (turn right at Hyde Park Blvd.). From the Loop, take the Metra (Randolph St. station on Michigan Ave. to stops at 57th and 59th Sts.). By bus, take the #6 Jeffery Express, which you can catch in the Loop on State St. For more information, call the CTA/RTA at 773-836-7000, or visit the Web site at **http://www. transitchicago.com**.

COURSE

Starting at the base of the 57th Dr. overhead bridge, you'll step into a vital stretch of Chicago history as you pass the Museum of Science and Industry (on your left). Follow the sidewalk along 57th Dr., which blends (left) into Cornell Dr. Veer right to 59th St., where you will cross Stony Island, and go left over to the East Midway Plaisance. Head under the Metra tracks and follow the sidewalk westward down this gorgeous 1.2-mile stretch of green field (or white, depending on the season), which was the home of the first Ferris wheel (constructed for the 1893 World Columbian Exposition).

At the corner of 59th and Woodlawn, note the neo-Gothic Rockefeller Memorial Chapel (named for U of C founder John D. Rockefeller). At the end of the Midway Plaisance, cross the street (to the right) to view

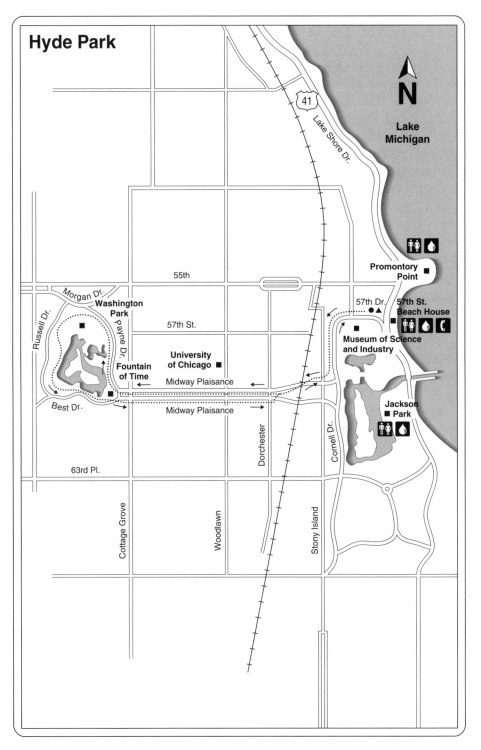

Hyde Park

Lake Michigan

41

Lake Shore Dr.

N

55th

Morgan Dr.

Washington
Park

Russell Dr.

Payne Dr.

57th St.

Fountain
of Time

University
of Chicago

Midway Plaisance

Best Dr.

Midway Plaisance

63rd Pl.

Cottage Grove

Woodlawn

Dorchester

Stony Island

Cornell Dr.

Promontory
Point

57th Dr.

57th St.
Beach House

Museum of Science
and Industry

Jackson
Park

the Fountain of Time. Considered one of the great concrete sculptures in North America (120 feet long and 20 feet high), the 100 figures all connect in one long sweep before cloaked Father Time.

Now you are officially in Washington Park, which may seem familiar to you if you've ever had the good fortune to run in New York's Central Park. Why? Frederick Law Olmsted designed both parks. The roads circling both have the same deceiving slight incline, and both include beautiful lagoons. I chose the outer path that's closer to the streets (Payne Dr. to Morgan Dr. to Russell Dr. and finally Best Dr.) to get more mileage. When you come back to the south side of the Fountain of Time, cross the street to the West Midway Plaisance and follow the sidewalk to Blackstone St., where you can cut across the street (left) in front of an equestrian statue honoring Thomas Masaryk (a professor at U of C who returned to Czechoslovakia to become the first president). Head back along the original course to finish this loop at the lakefront.

HYDE PARK HIGHLIGHTS

Two local races highlight the Gothic beauty of Hyde Park and are well worth checking out.

Each spring, the Gargoyle Gallop 8K takes runners through a figure-eight loop tour of Jackson Park. This race has a reputation for unique t-shirts (one of the few I've saved!) and original awards (many racers have thrown in an extra surge to ensure winning a coveted gargoyle trophy). For information, call 312-674-2334. In addition to being a cofounder of the race, Bill Gerstein, executive director of Partners in Community Development, has led a 20-year quest to bring a first-rate running track to the area and is thrilled to finally have the funding for one. The new track will be built at Stony Island, between 62nd and 63rd Sts.

Come September, join over 4,000 runners for the Chicago Half-Marathon. A relatively new race, this 13.1-mile trek showcases both boulevards and is an excellent warm-up for marathon season. The youth mile, kid's dash, and variety of nearby museums make this a great family-oriented event. For information, call 773-929-6072.

Trivia question answer: *When Harry Met Sally.*

INDIAN BOUNDARY TRAIL NORTH

14.5 MILES	TRAIL 👫 💧	SCENERY RATING	🌲🌲🌲🌲🌲
		HILL RATING	

Along the banks of the Des Plaines River, parallel to the western border of Chicago, is a boundary drawn up in the early 1800s with the Potawatomi Indians. This path crosses that line and is a pleasant surprise for urban dwellers. The best aspect is its proximity. A mere 45-minute bike ride from the North Side makes this route a must for cross-trainers or triathletes. One caveat—while it's easy to picture Indian villages along the river's edge, the occasional thunder of a plane landing at nearby O'Hare Airport brings you back to the 21st century.

ACCESS

By car, take Irving Park Rd. via Lake Shore Dr. (approximately 10.5 miles) or I-90 to Cumberland Ave. South. At the Cumberland Ave./Irving Park Rd. junction go through the light heading west past several groves until you see a gold Horse Trail sign on the right. Park in Grove #15 on the left side (most convenient).

By CTA, take the Blue line (O'Hare) to Cumberland. It's a short run to Bryn Mawr. Turn west for a half mile to catch the trail (close to the 2.2-mile mark) at the corner of Bryn Mawr and East River Rd.

COURSE

From Grove #15, as always, use caution crossing the street before heading onto this dirt trail. At the .8-mile fork, keep right by the construction area. A bit further, the trail narrows considerably, and you can keep going straight and through the parking area or follow the single track (to the right). Cross Lawrence Ave., or turn right and head down a gravel slope under the viaduct. From here, the bridle path widens to accommodate three runners abreast. Other than a few roots and a fallen tree, it's smooth going. At 1.9 miles, hang a left over an old stone bridge. With the Des Plaines River to your left and preserve parking areas to your right, you shouldn't get lost. At 2.2 miles, the path

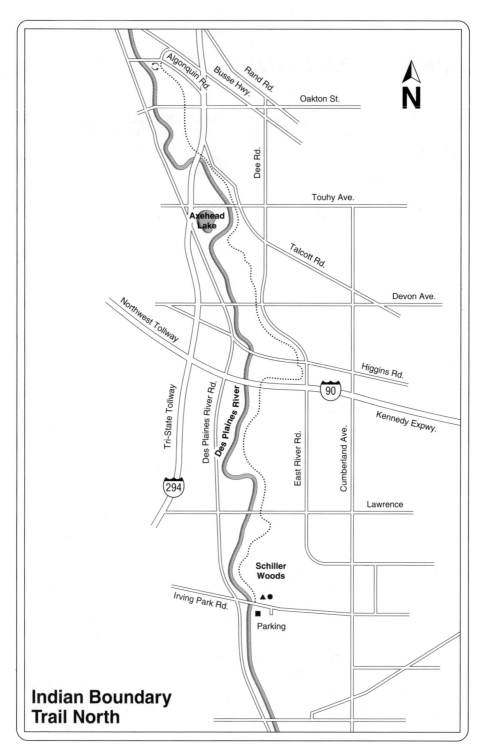

**Indian Boundary
Trail North**

splits around a big oak tree. Stay to the left until you reach the Kennedy Expwy./Northwest Tollway underpass at 2.5 miles. Follow the trail along these two dark (muddy) underpasses, whereupon the path becomes very narrow and confusing. If you go left, it winds around the cemetery fence (path is a U-shape) or go to the right up the embankment to a gravel road. Take the single-track path along the edge of the cemetery, or follow the gravel road a half mile around the bend to the alternate path on the left. Cross at Higgins Rd., and from there, the path is easy to follow. You'll know you've reached the end at Algonquin Rd. when you see a large sign for the United Methodist Campground.

Alternate route: For a 5-mile out-and-back, run from Irving Park Rd. to the Kennedy Expwy./Northwest Tollway.

FOOT NOTES

Wet weather is a hindrance, causing flooding and muddy conditions, but this course offers a forgiving surface. If the first section is under water, you can find additional parking on the north side of Irving Park Rd., such as Grove #3 and # 4, or Robinson Reserve off Lawrence Ave. has parking near the trail.

TIP

You might crave the intensity that comes with a race; if so, try the Rock 'N Sole Trail Challenge, which begins and ends in Schiller Woods. For information, call 773-868-0893.

MAGNIFICENT MILE

1 MILE	ROAD 👫 💧 📞	SCENERY RATING	
		HILL RATING	

ACCESS

Michigan Ave./Oak St.: By car, take Lake Shore Dr. to Oak St. You'll find metered parking on side streets. By CTA, take the Red line to Clark/Division St. or Chicago Ave. and go east. By bus, #145, #146, #147, and #151 all stop here. For more information, call the CTA/RTA at 312-836-7000 or visit their Web site at **http://www.transitchicago.com**.

Michigan Ave./Chicago River: By car, take Lake Shore Dr. to Illinois St./Michigan Ave. or lower Wacker Dr. By CTA, take the Red line to Grand Ave. By bus, see preceding instructions.

COURSE

Don't try this for a PR, but rather at a leisurely pace early in the day, which will allow you to do a little window shopping in some of Chicago's most exclusive stores. Starting at Oak St. (on the edge of the Gold Coast) you can't miss the marquee of the historic Drake Hotel for the transition from beach to retail mecca. As you head south, you'll pass by some of Chicago's favorite tourist attractions: John Hancock Center and Water Tower Place (shopping center) with the Historic Water Tower and Pumping Station (sole survivors of the great fire of 1871) by Chicago Ave. This is an important crossroads to remember. If you go directly east, you'll pass the Museum of Contemporary Art, where you can usually find a thought-provoking exhibit and a cafe with reasonably priced sandwiches, but what you'll appreciate as a runner is the four-lane, quarter-mile track behind the museum in Lake Shore Playground Park.

Back on Michigan Ave., between Superior and Huron Sts., you can't miss Chicago Place with its flagship store, Saks Fifth Avenue. The Terra Museum of American Art is on the next block, and the Ohio St./Grand Ave. section has several megathemed stores. You can take either of these streets east to the lakefront path via the underpass. Just before the

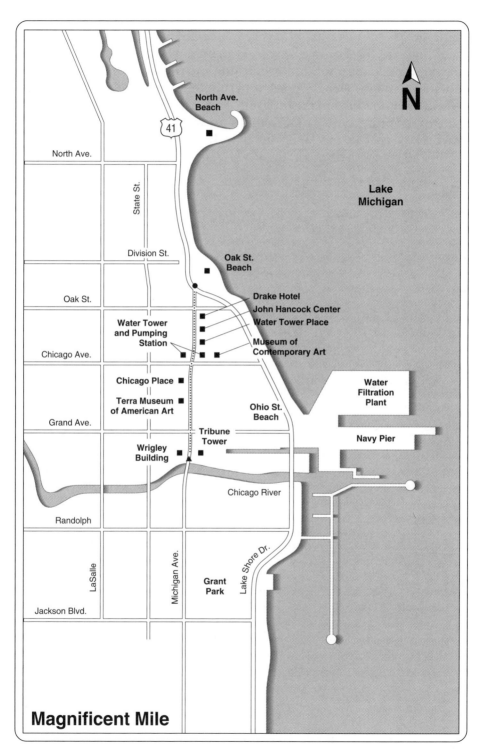

Magnificent Mile

North Ave. Beach

41

North Ave.

State St.

Division St.

Oak St. Beach

Oak St.

Drake Hotel

John Hancock Center

Water Tower Place

Water Tower and Pumping Station

Museum of Contemporary Art

Chicago Ave.

Chicago Place

Terra Museum of American Art

Grand Ave.

Ohio St. Beach

Water Filtration Plant

Navy Pier

Tribune Tower

Wrigley Building

Chicago River

Randolph

LaSalle

Michigan Ave.

Lake Shore Dr.

Grant Park

Jackson Blvd.

Lake Michigan

N

Chicago River bridge are two very important landmarks, the Wrigley Building and the Tribune Tower. I ran by the latter for years before a friend stopped me one Sunday morning and pointed out that along the outside wall 140 labeled stones from ruins and monuments all over the world are imbedded in the building. Here ends the mile. On the south side of the bridge you can take the stairs to lower Wacker Dr. and the Riverwalk east to the lakefront path by the Columbia Yacht Club. Safety alert: use caution on the Riverwalk.

TIP

Several training groups and Run Chicago hold track workouts at Lake Shore Playground Park.

NORTH SIDE LANDMARKS RUN

| 4.25 MILES | ROAD | SCENERY RATING | |
| | | HILL RATING | |

If you're interested in finding some neat nooks and crannies, try this interesting jaunt away from the lakefront congestion—you'll especially appreciate it if you're a history or architecture buff.

ACCESS

By car, take Lake Shore Dr. to the parking lots in Lincoln Park at Irving Park Rd. or Montrose. By CTA, take the Red line to Sheridan or Addison; via bus take #145, #146, or #155 along Sheridan Rd. or #22 or #36 on Clark St., getting off at Irving Park Rd.

COURSE

From the lakefront, head west on Irving Park Rd. for one mile to the corner of Clark and Irving Park Rd. Here you'll find Graceland Cemetery, a cornucopia of Chicago history. Get a free map at the main office, and among the massive oaks and maples you can find the final resting places of Chicago tycoons like Cyrus McCormick, inventor of the grain harvesting machine, Marshall Field ("the Merchant Prince"), and architect Louis Sullivan. From here, go back down Irving Park Rd., turn right before the "el" tracks at Seminary St., and follow the narrow strip along Kelly Park past Grace St. to Waveland St. Aha! You're at Gate K of Wrigley Field, home of the Chicago Cubs, an awesome sight (even if you don't have blue blood). It's worth the time to take the short jog around the block and check out the famous marquee on the corner of Clark and Addison or see if the flags flying in the breeze display the W for a win or L for a loss. Once you're back at Gate K, head back down Seminary to Grace St.; about 20 yards to your right is Alta Vista Ter., a historic landmark since 1972. What makes this "block of 40 doors" so unique is that each Victorian townhouse, built at the turn of the century, mirrors the one on the opposite side of the street.

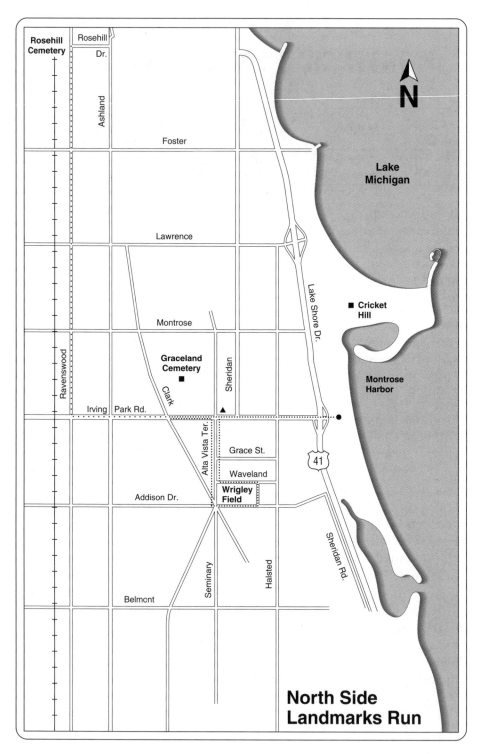

Rosehill
Cemetery

Rosehill
Dr.

Ashland

Foster

Lawrence

Montrose

Ravenswood

Graceland
Cemetery

Clark

Sheridan

Irving Park Rd.

Alta Vista Ter.

Grace St.

Waveland

Wrigley
Field

Addison Dr.

Seminary

Halsted

Belmont

N

Lake
Michigan

Lake Shore Dr.

Cricket
Hill

Montrose
Harbor

41

Sheridan Rd.

**North Side
Landmarks Run**

Additional course: Not tired? Head back down Irving Park Rd., go west for about one mile, and turn right at Ravenswood. This street runs parallel to the Metra tracks, and here one can find several factories and artist studios. Keeping to the center of the street is easier on the knees because it's quite curved. Within two miles, look above the tracks to your left and you'll see, in the distance, a flag atop a structure that looks astonishingly like the Water Tower. The Rosehill Cemetery entrance is made of limestone like the Water Tower and was designed by the same architect. The sign out front says "No Jogging," so please adhere to this, but ask for a brochure at the main desk, and you can find the final resting places for Avery Brudage (director of the International Olympic Committee and U.S. Olympic Association from 1952 to 1972) and Ignaz Schwinn (the man behind the bike) among some beautiful sculptures.

TIP

A great breakfast spot along the additional course route is Pauline's. This diner, on the corner of Ravenswood and Balmoral, is filled with 1950s memorabilia. For information, call 773-561-8573.

THE NORTH

1. Evanston
2. Green Bay Trail
3. Home "Eco" Economist
4. Lake Forest
5. North Branch Trail North
6. North Branch Trail South (Caldwell Woods)
7. North Shore Channel
8. Old School Forest Preserve

Chicago's northern suburbs, more commonly known as the North Shore, are famous for celebrity residents, exclusive schools, and coveted waterfront property. You don't have to be wealthy, however, to enjoy the wealth of running options.

Evanston, just north of the city, can be explored via its lakefront. You'll run through Northwestern University and turn around at a visually stunning house of worship. On the western outskirts of Evanston, follow the North Shore Channel trail (built to absorb the overflow from the North Branch of the Chicago River). This trail can link you to the North Branch Trail South (less than four miles to the west) or to the Green Bay Trail (a little over a mile to the north).

Both the North Branch and Green Bay trails pass through several suburbs, offering many access points. Run these courses and make it a day-long outing, including stops at the Chicago Botanic Garden at the northern end of the North Branch Trail and the Ravinia Festival in Highland Park (conveniently located next to the Green Bay Trail).

Check out the Lake Forest run for a winding course through the city and along the beachfront. Further northwest is the Home "Eco" Economist run in Barrington. If you're in shape and have some miles under your belt, this is one of the most challenging runs in the guide. The Old School Forest Preserve offers a variety of loops in a well-maintained stretch of woods, perfect for runners of all abilities.

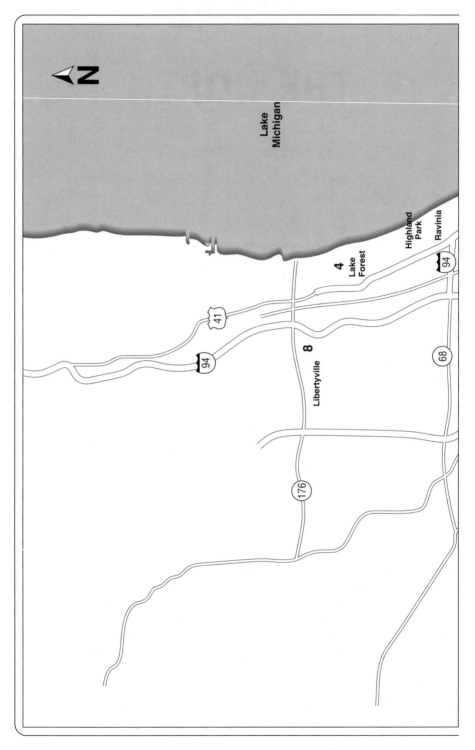

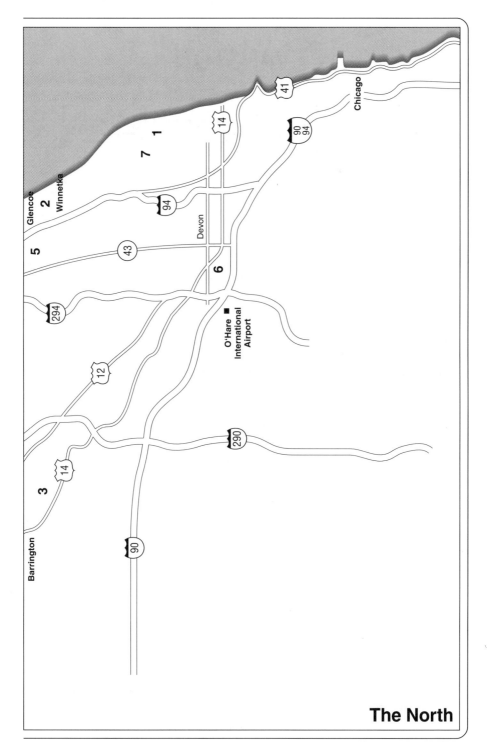

The North

EVANSTON

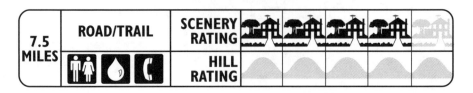

7.5 MILES	ROAD/TRAIL	SCENERY RATING	
		HILL RATING	

You might call this run *Heavenston* for a variety of reasons: it has beaches, glorious lakefront views, and a jaunt around prestigious Northwestern University, with a turnaround by the impressive Bahá'í Temple. Don't feel guilty if you want to stop and absorb the sights; there's plenty to see—enough to stop any runner in his or her tracks.

ACCESS

By car, take Lake Shore Dr. (north) to Hollywood, then follow Sheridan Rd. to Greenleaf St. (right) to Lake Shore Blvd./Elliot Park. (Note: Greenleaf St. is between Main St. and Dempster St., not to be confused with Greenleaf St. in Rogers Park.) You'll find plenty of street parking. By Metra, take the Union Pacific North line to Main St. and go east to the lakefront path. By CTA: on weekends, take the Red line to Howard St. and transfer to the Purple line (Evanston Express); during the week, catch the Purple line (Evanston Express) to Main St. For CTA/Metra information, call 312-836-7000, or visit **http://www.metrarail.com**.

COURSE

Start at Greenleaf St./Elliot Park by the restrooms and water fountain. Follow the crushed gravel path north to the Northwestern University campus (1 mile), where it turns into a paved bike trail. Follow the trail to the right, around the parking area, where you might find yourself doing the "hello dance" (frantic waving to ward off occasional divebombing birds). Cross the bridge and keep to your right, following the path closest to the lakefront. You'll be greeted by either a refreshing breeze or a chilly northern blast, depending on the season. On a clear day you can view the Chicago skyline. Follow the curve past the soccer field, and at the stop sign (2.1 miles) turn right past the Henry Crown Sports Pavilion. Then turn left at Lincoln St. and right at Sheridan Rd., following the tree-lined sidewalk past the Grosse Point Lighthouse (a

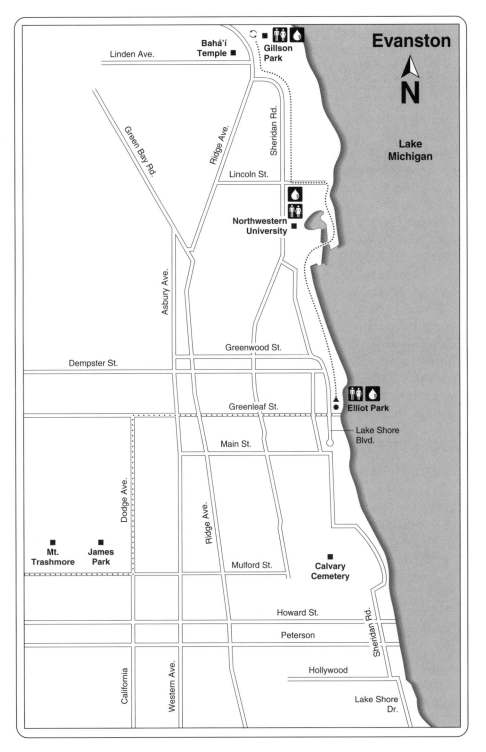

historical landmark built in 1873). Follow Sheridan Rd. as it turns left, then go right when it merges with Ridge Ave. (3.1 miles). Shortly, you'll enter Wilmette village limits, and on the opposite side of the street view the majestic Bahá'í Temple with its enormous white dome—an awe-inspiring sight no matter how many times you run this course. Since 1953, this house of worship, with its unique architecture and lush gardens, has drawn thousands of visitors. Beyond that is the turn-around—the entrance to Gillson Park (3.7 miles). Water and restrooms are available between the parks and the university.

Additional routes: If you're feeling ambitious and want to tack on another 3 miles, check out "Mt. Trashmore." Northwestern Wildcat football players and Evanstonians have conquered this popular sledding hill; it's great for rigorous repeats and is highly recommended by Coach Pat Savage of the Niles West/Oakton Runners Club. Take Greenleaf St. to Dodge Ave., go left to Mulford St., then turn right to the back section of James Park.

If you want to add some miles, explore Northwestern University's beautifully landscaped campus and admire the magnificent homes along Sheridan Rd., or head south through Rogers Park (use caution, however; this is not the safest area). The path is interrupted by sidewalks and streets, and the section by Calvary Cemetery is narrow. If you follow Sheridan Rd. south, you can pick up the Chicago Lakefront path at Hollywood (see page 5).

FOOT NOTES

Hook up with the Evanston Running Club for this course at 6:30 P.M. on Mondays (during daylight savings time—April through October). While the Evanston lakefront path may not be as long as Lincoln Park, club president Keith Holzmueller will attest to its many beautiful sights, especially the view of the skyline from the south end of the Northwestern landfill. Winter weather doesn't deter this club, either! When the windchill dips below zero, you can join them at the Evanston High School indoor track and perfect your technique at their "Wintervals" workouts.

TIP

Popular local races include the Active Endeavors Frozen 5K (March): call 773-281-8100 or 847-869-7070; and the Arbor Day Five (April): call 847-448-8046.

GREEN BAY TRAIL

9.4 MILES	TRAIL	SCENERY RATING		HILL RATING

The Green Bay Trail is a beautiful path for runners and walkers alike, as it takes you through some of the most exclusive neighborhoods of the northern suburbs. This heavily shaded route is cushioned by crushed limestone, and much of it is hidden from the busy streets.

ACCESS

Easily accessible by the Metra train; exit at any of the stops between Wilmette and Highland Park. By car, you can access the trail along Green Bay Rd. There is plenty of metered parking along the route and some street parking. Just be aware that some spots require a permit.

COURSE

The south end of this trail begins in Wilmette at Lake Ave., just on the east side of Green Bay Rd. and the Metra train tracks. The trail heads north, following the train tracks and Green Bay Rd., through the north suburbs of Kenilworth, Winnetka, Glencoe, and Highland Park. It actually continues up to Highwood; however, our map only goes as far as downtown Highland Park. As you enter the Winnetka part of the trail, this path will take you down alongside the Metra tracks, which are below the suburban streets. At times you will feel lost in this cavern—surrounded on both sides, with only the sky above, train tracks on your left, and trees on either side as your scenery.

As you continue north, the trail takes you through downtown Glencoe. At approximately 6.9 miles into your journey, you will cross the entrance to Ravinia, which is a beautiful outdoor amphitheater. Ravinia offers live music nightly, ranging from classical to rock and roll. There is outdoor seating during the summer months, and lawn seats are usually no more than $6 per person. Finally, the trail heads into downtown Highland Park, where you will find many areas to rest, eat, or even continue further north into Highwood if you are interested.

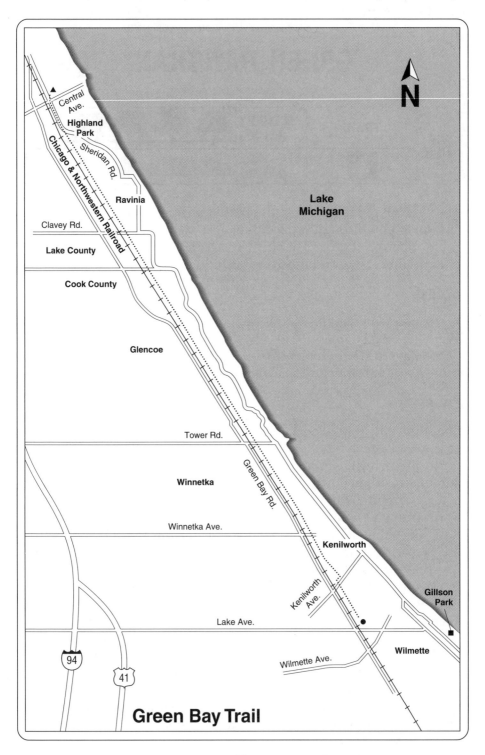

N

Central Ave.

Highland Park

Sheridan Rd.

Chicago & Northwestern Railroad

Ravinia

Lake Michigan

Clavey Rd.

Lake County

Cook County

Glencoe

Tower Rd.

Green Bay Rd.

Winnetka

Winnetka Ave.

Kenilworth

Kenilworth Ave.

Gillson Park

Lake Ave.

94

Wilmette

41

Wilmette Ave.

Green Bay Trail

HOME "ECO" ECONOMIST

10.6-MILE LOOP	ROAD	SCENERY RATING	
	💧	HILL RATING	

If you complain to your East- and West-Coast friends that you can't run hills because Chicago is so flat, stop and mark this page—you'll be guaranteed never to say that again. Rolling hills, mingled with beautiful countryside estates, lakes, and horse farms, provide quite a challenge. Run here and you'll develop the stamina and confidence to tackle the likes of Boston's Heartbreak Hill or Oregon's Hood to Coast.

ACCESS

Just 35 miles northwest of the city. By car, take I-90/I-94 north, then take the I-90 tollway to Rte. 53 (north) Rolling Meadows exit and head north to Rte. 14 (Northwest Hwy.). Traffic will be slow through Palatine, and shortly after you pass Thunderbird Country Club (to your right) is the Home Economist store and parking lot. By Metra, take the Union Pacific Northwest line to Spring St./Park Ave. (less than a mile from the trailhead). For more information, call the CTA/RTA at 312-836-7000, or visit their Web site at **http://www.metrarail.com**.

COURSE

Start at the Home Economist store on the corner of Rte. 14 (Northwest Hwy.) and Hillside Ave., heading immediately across Rte. 14 and the railroad tracks, where you pass Baker Lake and head through a residential neighborhood. After the stoplight at Hough St. (Rte. 59), you'll spot Evergreen Cemetery at the end of Hillside Ave. Turn left onto Dundee Ln., then take a quick right on Tower Rd. for one block. Turn left on Country Dr., which leads to the most picturesque part of the course, Otis Rd. For the next 3.5 to 6.5 miles, you'll run on Old Sutton Rd., Donlea Rd., and a busy Lake Cook Rd. (please use extra caution here). During warm weather, you can stop at the Countryside School and use the drinking fountain down by the tennis courts (note: the only water stop available). You can be an Honest Abe with your

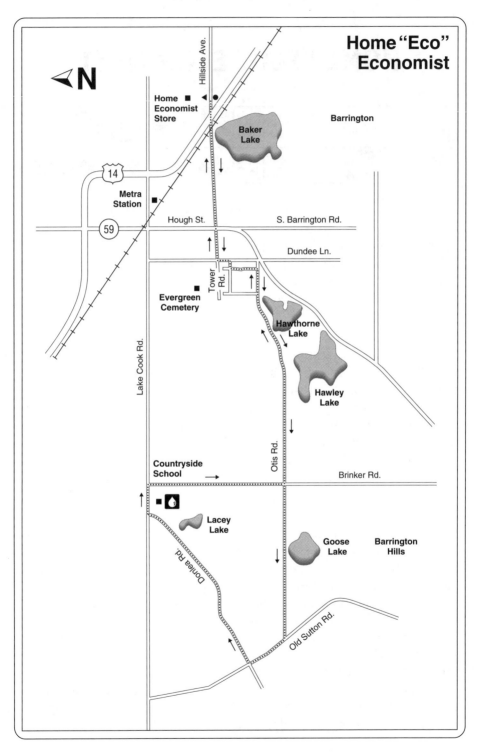

mileage, going back up to Lake Cook Rd. and turning right, or, if you need to get a drink, cut though the school grounds to Brinker Rd. Follow this to Otis Rd. and back to the start. You will get a slight break after you cross back over Rte. 59 on Hillside Ave., because it's pretty much downhill.

FOOT NOTES

One of the largest local clubs, the Alpine Runners (see page 141), sponsors organized marathon training and fun runs in nearby Lake Zurich with excellent maps and course directions. Although this isn't an Alpine-sponsored event, you can find many competitive members and triathletes at the Home Eco run every Sunday at 7 A.M. sharp! And believe me, it's a snap making it on time, because driving at this hour is hassle free. One final word: Beth Onines, marathon training coordinator for the Alpine Runners, advises that "this is not for the inexperienced runner."

LAKE FOREST

6.5-MILE LOOP	ROAD	SCENERY RATING	
	🚻 💧 ☎	HILL RATING	

Each Saturday at 8 A.M., join an enthusiastic group of Lake Forest/Lake Bluff runners at the train station across from the historic Market Square. Built in 1916, it's the first planned shopping center in the United States. The course is just the recipe you need to start your weekend: add some new folks, dish a little gossip, sprinkle in a scenic neighborhood, glaze by a nice stretch of beachfront, toss in an uphill and maybe a glimpse of a celebrity (many well-to-do types reside here), and blend it all together for a truly pleasurable run.

ACCESS

Just 30 miles north of the city. From the Loop, take I-94 north to Rte. 41. Exit at Deerpath (right) and go east a little over a mile to the Lake Forest train station (also known as the east station). On Saturday mornings, the Metra Union Pacific/North line #305 leaves downtown Chicago at 6:30 A.M., and you can pick it up at several locations heading north, arriving at the start of this course by 7:35 A.M. Save money and get a $5 weekend pass. For more CTA/Metra information, call 312-836-7000, or visit **http://www.metrarail.com**. There is plenty of parking around the station or Market Square.

COURSE

From the train station, head right on Westminster and then right again on Lake Rd., which runs parallel to the lakefront. As you head south through Forest Park, take a sharp left down a steep descent to the scenic beachfront. Head through the parking lot (can be slippery during winter and spring, so watch your step). As the saying goes, what comes down must go up, so at the opposite end of the park you'll turn right to tackle the uphill. Lower your arms and lift your knees for a vertical climb sure to slow even six-minute milers. This next section can be confusing as you head back into the residential streets of Lake Rd.,

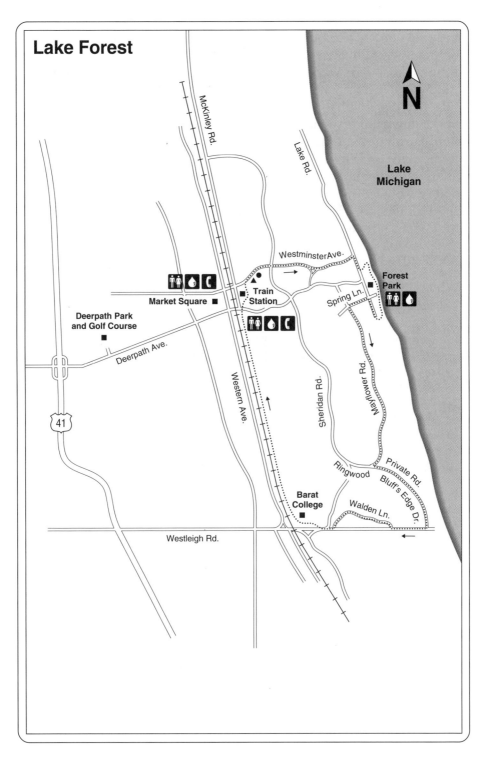

heading north. Take a left on Spring Ln. and follow it south to the end of Mayflower Rd. Here you take a sharp left onto a private road at the Ringwood St. sign, which leads you toward a gorgeous ravine and over the newly restored historic Walden/Bluff's Edge bridge to Bluff's Edge Dr. Local club runner Mike Koob spearheaded the bridge project, and fellow runners helped raise the money necessary for its renovation. Turn right onto Westleigh Rd. and take a slight detour around it to the right on Walden Ln. before coming back to the Westleigh and Sheridan Rd. intersection. This is a busy street, so please use caution before cutting straight through the parking lot at Barat College. Turn right for the last 1.5-mile stretch on the paved Lake Forest/Lake Bluff trail back to the train station.

FOOT NOTES

While a bit craggy at spots, the Lake Forest trail (which follows the old North Shore rail line) goes all the way north into Wisconsin or south to the Highland Park bike path. Other spots favored by many locals are the winding dirt trails in the open lands area near the Deerpath Park and Golf Course (on the north side of Deerpath just after you exit Rte. 41).

TIP

In need of a haircut? Inside the train station you'll find Ruffolo's Barber Shop, open six days a week from 7:30 A.M. to 5 P.M. This old-fashioned shop is straight out of a Norman Rockwell painting.

NORTH BRANCH TRAIL NORTH

20.1 MILES	PAVED TRAIL	SCENERY RATING	🌳 🌳 🌳 🌳 🌳
👫 💧 ☎		HILL RATING	

People begin running for any number of motives, but we stick to it for one basic reason—to find out who we really are.

—George Sheehan

Gardens have long been a source of inspiration and contemplation, which is why this destination run to or from the Chicago Botanic Garden is treasured by many. It's the third most-visited public garden in the nation.

ACCESS

Northern trailhead: Chicago Botanic Garden. From the Loop, take I-94 north to Rte. 41. Exit at Dundee Rd. or Lake Cook Rd. (east). By Metra, take the Union Pacific North line to Glencoe and go north about a quarter of a mile to Dundee Rd., which is close to the Skokie Lagoons. The Chicago Botanic Garden is approximately a half mile from the Braeside stop. For Metra information, call 312-836-7000, or visit their Web site at **http://www.metrarail.com**. By PACE bus, take #213 to Green Bay Rd. For PACE information, call the same number as for the Metra, or visit the Web site at **http://www.pacebus.com**.
Southern trailhead: See North Branch Trail South (Caldwell Woods).

COURSE

This twisting, winding, paved trail parallel to the north branch of the Chicago River is perfect for both long-distance training and shorter runs. With so many access points, you can take several weekends to explore the whole trail. Prairie fields, picnic groves with water pumps, and golf courses dot the way. A few busy roads require use of traffic

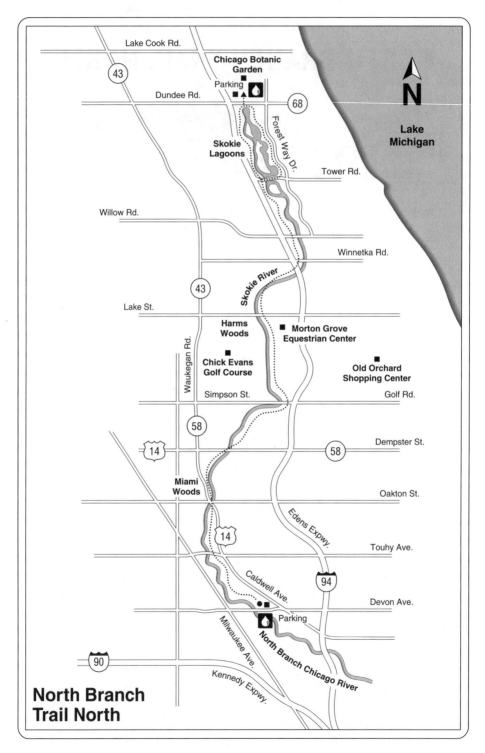

Lake Cook Rd.

Chicago Botanic
Garden

Parking

43

Dundee Rd.

68

N

Lake
Michigan

Forest Way Dr.

Skokie
Lagoons

Tower Rd.

Willow Rd.

Winnetka Rd.

Skokie River

43

Lake St.

Harms
Woods

Morton Grove
Equestrian Center

Waukegan Rd.

Chick Evans
Golf Course

Old Orchard
Shopping Center

Simpson St.

Golf Rd.

58

14

58

Dempster St.

Miami
Woods

Oakton St.

Edens Expwy.

14

Touhy Ave.

94

Caldwell Ave.

Devon Ave.

Parking

Milwaukee Ave.

North Branch Chicago River

90

Kennedy Expwy.

North Branch
Trail North

buttons. Two overpasses, one at Oakton St. (4 miles) and one at Lake St. (9 miles), provide inclines; otherwise, it's quite flat. Several dirt equestrian trails run parallel to the path (you can't miss Morton Grove Equestrian Center near Harms Woods). If you continue north after Lake St., keep right at the fork crossing Harms Rd. or you'll end up at Winnetka Rd. Willow Rd. marks the southern tip of the Skokie Lagoons and is surrounded by a lovely sedge meadow. *Skokie* is an Indian word meaning swamp, but this lagoon is hardly swamplike from the confines of the trail. If your aim is to do the lagoon loop, street parking is available along Forest Way. Across Dundee Rd. is the service entrance into the Chicago Botanic Garden. Follow the runner/walker path on the left side of the road; it leads to the Gateway Center (maps, water, food, restrooms). Note: eventually this trail connects with the Green Bay Trail.

FOOT NOTES

What better way to end a tempo run or leisurely weekend jaunt than the Chicago Botanic Garden? This 385-acre horticultural heaven features 23 unique gardens (my favorites include the rose, Japanese, and English walled gardens). Open all year except Christmas Day; for more information, call 847-835-5440, or visit the Web site at **http://www.chicago-botanic.org**. Also, the Food for Thought Cafe in the Gateway Center sells sport drinks and sport bars.

NORTH BRANCH TRAIL SOUTH (CALDWELL WOODS)

3.9 MILES	TRAIL [icons]	SCENERY RATING	[4.5 trees]
		HILL RATING	[hills]

Foresight is the term that comes to mind when describing the Cook County Forest Preserves. Someone had the vision to set aside land for outdoor recreational use and created a gem of a trail surrounded by nature, just footsteps from the hustle and bustle of the busy city and suburbs.

ACCESS

From the Loop, take I-94 north to Rte. 41. Exit at Caldwell Ave. (west) to Devon Ave. Park at the trailhead in Groves #1, 2, or 3 near the Devon Ave./Milwaukee Ave. intersection. For biathletes and triathletes, try riding your bike up Elston St. to Milwaukee Ave. and turn right at Devon Ave. By CTA, take the Blue line–Jefferson Park and run approximately 2 miles north on Milwaukee to Devon. By Metra, take the Union Pacific North line to Edgebrook, which is by the Devon/Caldwell intersection. For CTA/Metra information, call 312-836-7000, or visit their Web site at **http://www.metrarail.com**.

COURSE

From the parking lot, head to the right down a small hill onto the paved trail, where you will cross a bridge. On the other side, you will see a large map detailing the North Branch Trail, which marks its official start. Keep left as the trail winds through meadows and nicely shaded stretches north to Touhy Ave. It can be quite active on the weekends and is popular for runners with baby joggers, but isn't too crowded. This trail continues north to the Chicago Botanic Garden.

Alternate route: Add on an additional 2.4 miles by turning right at the map board for an out-and-back extension past the Bunker Hill Prairie to the Caldwell Ave./Devon Ave. intersection.

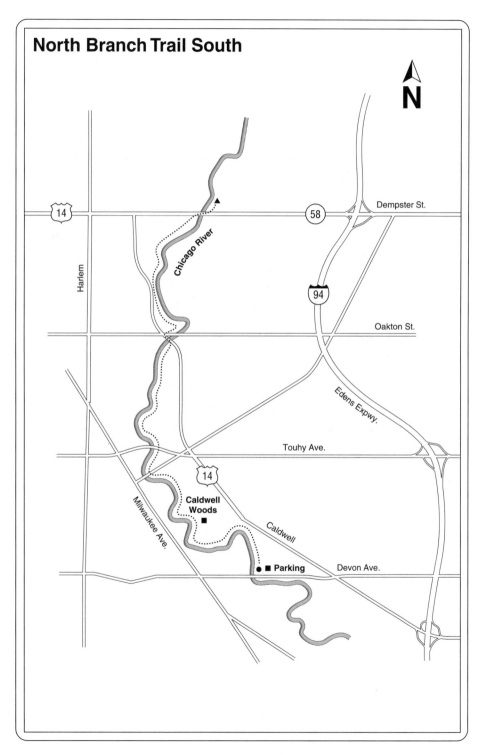

North Branch Trail South

N

14

Chicago River

58 Dempster St.

Harlem

94

Oakton St.

Edens Expwy.

Touhy Ave.

14

Caldwell
Woods

Milwaukee Ave.

Caldwell

■ Parking Devon Ave.

TIP

Afterward (*not* before), you must visit a classic Chicago hot dog stand, the Superdawg Drive-In (6363 N. Milwaukee Ave.). You can't miss Flaurie and Maurie, the "humanoid hot dogs," bidding you welcome from the rooftop. Try the superdawg with everything—fries and pickles—and the kosher hot dog served on a steamed bun.

EVEN FOOLS LIKE CALDWELL WOODS

When *Chicago Tribune* columnist Eric Zorn turned 40, he made a bold announcement to his readers that he was going to run the LaSalle Banks Chicago Marathon. Once you have it in print it's hard to back out, so he invited readers to join his running society, appropriately named FOOLS (For Once in Our Lives Society). A groundswell of folks responded; they trained together, kept in touch via the Internet, and some even finished together. Zorn's time was 4:31, and, needless to say (we all could have predicted this!), he's caught the bug and has continued to run. In 1999 he lowered his time to 4:22. Zorn trains here regularly; he especially likes the Miami Woods Prairie section after the Howard St. 3-mile mark. For FOOLS information, check out **http://www.runningfools.com**.

NORTH SHORE CHANNEL

4.8 MILES	PAVED TRAIL	SCENERY RATING		
		HILL RATING		

The North Shore Channel trail is a pleasant path starting at the northern tip of Chicago and traversing the north suburbs of Lincolnwood, Skokie, and Evanston. This paved trail is surrounded by grass on either side, with the Chicago River following you on the east side and McCormick Blvd. on the west side.

ACCESS

By car, the trail is accessible at any point along McCormick Blvd. between Devon Ave. and Green Bay Rd. There is parking at three points along the course, with the largest lot at the north end in Evanston at Bridge St. By Metra, go to Evanston Central stop and go south on Green Bay Rd. approximately a half mile to McCormick Blvd. Or take the CTA Purple line to Noyes stop and head west to trailhead.

COURSE

This suburban trail is fairly shaded at the Evanston end, which is where you will run through the Ladd Arboretum; however, the majority of the remaining trail is exposed to the sun. I recommend bringing along water for those hot and humid Chicago summer days. Restrooms are available at gas stations along the route. The middle portion of the trail winds through the Northshore Sculpture Park. The modern sculptures will help keep your mind occupied and also add some scenery to your run. This trail is also great for bikers and in-line skaters, because it is completely paved from Golf Rd. south, and there are plenty of bike racks and park benches along the course.

The North Shore Channel trail offers a wonderful running path and can easily connect to the Evanston, North Branch, and Green Bay trails.

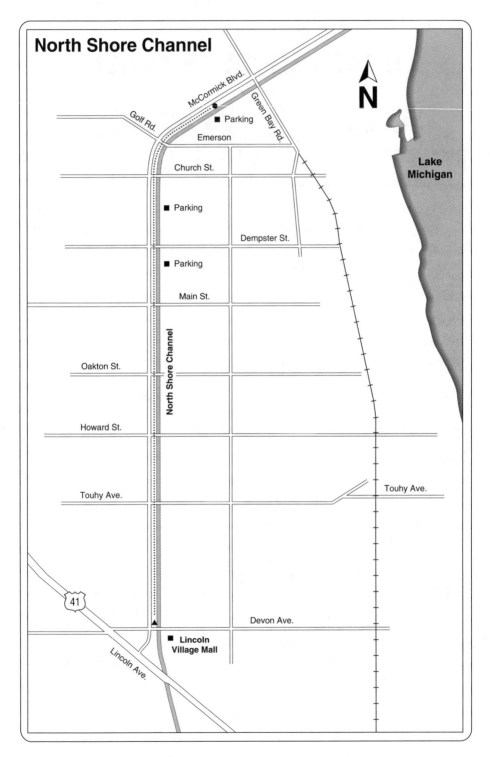

North Shore Channel

Golf Rd.

McCormick Blvd.

Green Bay Rd.

■ Parking

Emerson

Church St.

■ Parking

Dempster St.

■ Parking

Main St.

North Shore Channel

Oakton St.

Howard St.

Touhy Ave.

Touhy Ave.

Lake Michigan

N

41

Devon Ave.

■ **Lincoln Village Mall**

Lincoln Ave.

OLD SCHOOL FOREST PRESERVE

3.4-MILE LOOP	TRAIL	SCENERY RATING	
	🚻 💧 ☎	HILL RATING	

Principles in the school of running include vary your distances, don't be afraid to push yourself, and taper off before races. These well-groomed forest preserve trails offer a variety of lesson plans for every student of the sport.

ACCESS

From the Loop, take I-94 north; exit at Rte. 60. Go west to St. Mary's Rd. and turn right. The trailhead entrance is just north of Old School Rd. on the right. Park at the ranger station or follow the road to the Parking—Trails sign.

COURSE

Main route: Experience the wooded landscape and small prairies that color this 380-acre preserve with a loop that combines part of the 2.6-mile Des Plaines River Trail loop and most of the 1.2-mile Old School Lake loop. From the Ranger Station at the entrance, follow the crushed gravel path south for almost a mile where it splits. Follow Des Plaines River Trail sign north and cut through the parking lot by the old-fashioned fishing hole (stocked with bass and catfish) where the only bad news is its close proximity to a noisy I-94. The good news is that you can add some repeats up Sled Hill. Take the cutoff in the middle of the lake's west side and go through the parking lot to the far end where you can pick up the Des Plaines trail by the paved road, which leads back to the entrance by the Ranger Station.

Local running clubs recommend either continuing on the Des Plaines River Trail south through MacArthur Woods and Daniel Wright Woods to Rte. 22/Half Day Rd. or heading north, where it extends to the Wisconsin border. For information, call the Lake County Forest Preserve at 847-367-3675, or check out their Web site at **http://www.co.lake.il.us/forest**.

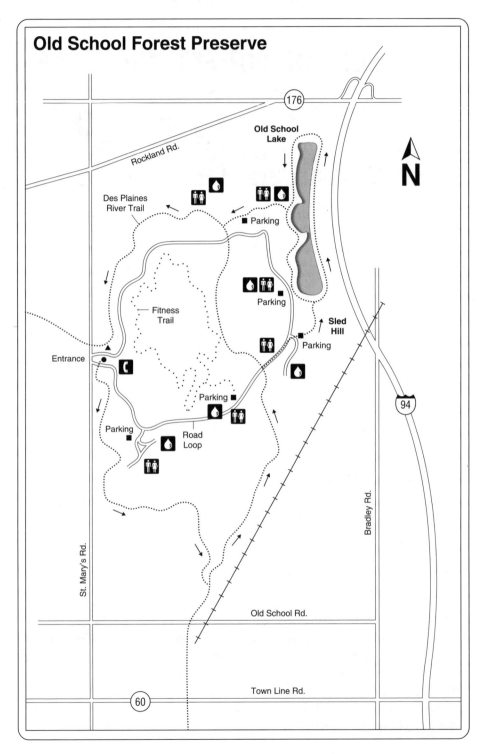

Old School Forest Preserve

176

Old School
Lake

Rockland Rd.

N

Des Plaines
River Trail

Parking

Parking

Fitness
Trail

Sled
Hill

Parking

Entrance

94

Parking

Parking

Road
Loop

Parking

Bradley Rd.

St. Mary's Rd.

Old School Rd.

Town Line Rd.

60

Additional routes: 1.5-mile road loop: asphalt. Marked one way; follow it to the right. 1.5-mile fitness loop: in the summer, a blanket of foliage shrouds this 3-foot-wide trail. Insect spray is recommended. Includes 19 workout stations—even a scaling wall! No bikes are allowed here.

FOOT NOTES

Each September, the Runner's Edge in Wilmette sponsors a half-marathon that starts and finishes here. For information, call 847-853-8531, or visit the Web site at **http://www.tre.com**. Also, this family-friendly preserve has a playground, shelters, clean restrooms, and even canine accessories—only on the north shore will you find biodegradable Mutt Mitts to pick up after your four-legged training companion.

TRAINING GROUND OF CHAMPIONS

Jenny Spangler made a mark for herself by leading from the front and upsetting the favorites for an impressive 2:29:54 victory in the 1996 U.S. Olympic Marathon trials. At 19 she captured the U.S. national junior marathon record in 2:33 and went on to qualify for two Olympic marathon trials. Jenny trains here all year round. During the winter, a typical workout includes 1-mile repeats with a half-mile recovery on the paved road loop. "Sometimes I will do a run on the trail and then finish up at Sled Hill with several repeats." Run Chicago coach Greg Domantay highly recommends these trails: "It's my favorite place to run." Even with a 22:47 8K PR, this University of Illinois cross country All-American takes time to enjoy the scenery: "I see more wildlife and witness changes throughout all four seasons."

THE WEST

According to family history, Papa Clarence Hemingway blew his trumpet on the porch to announce Ernest's birth on July 21, 1899.

—Ernest Hemingway Foundation of Oak Park

1. Blackwell Forest Preserve
2. Busse Woods
3. Fox River Trail Middle Section (St. Charles, Geneva, and Batavia)
4. Great Western Trail (Western Branch)
5. Great Western Trail (Eastern Branch)
6. Illinois Prairie Path Main Stem (Wheaton to Elmhurst)
7. Illinois Prairie Path Northwest Branch (Wheaton to Elgin)
8. Illinois Prairie Path Southwest Branch (Wheaton to Aurora)
9. Oak Park

After I started exploring some of these trails, I felt like getting on a porch somewhere and blowing a horn to alert non-west-suburban runners to these trails! Run these and I'm sure you'll have some endorphins kick in, too.

The Oak Park run is the closest western route to the city and is filled with historical landmarks related to literary and architectural icons Ernest Hemingway and Frank Lloyd Wright. Hear the phrase "rails-to-trails" and you might envision cowboys and gold mines. Okay, so we're only in the *Mid*west and I doubt if you'll stumble on any gold nuggets, but the Illinois Prairie Paths and the Great Western Trails, part of the rails-to-trails movement, are gems. Not only are they well

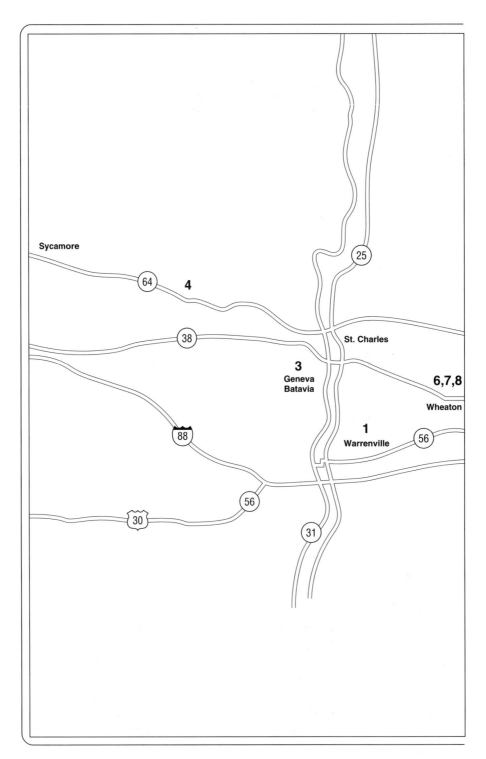

Sycamore

64 **4**

38

25

St. Charles

3
Geneva
Batavia

6,7,8

Wheaton

88

1
Warrenville

56

56

30

31

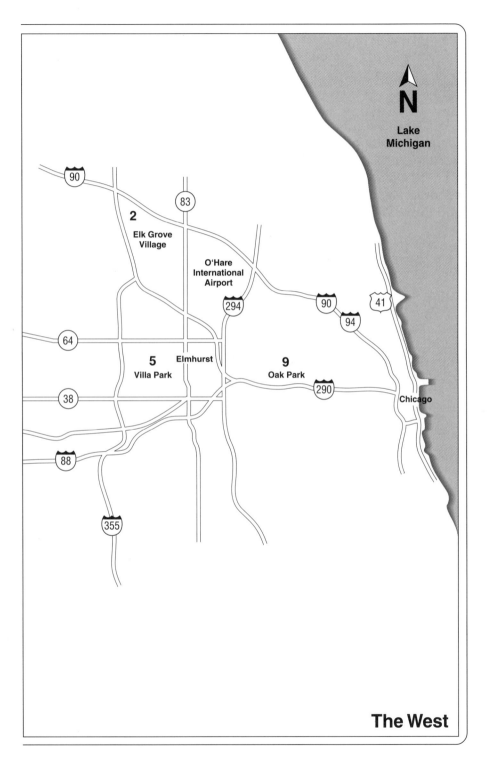

The West

marked and very popular with long-distance runners, but they're also perfect for cross training on bikes in the summer or cross-country skiing in the winter.

The Fox River Trail extends from Aurora to Crystal Lake; over 36 miles of paved trail follow the scenic riverfront. Due to space constraints, we only have one entry, which is similar to an appetizer—there's enough information to get you going, but I'm confident you'll want to check out the whole course.

For two loop courses that will take you through shaded woods and tall prairie grasses and past some great fishing spots and a herd of elk, add Busse Woods and the Blackwell Forest Preserve to your list.

BLACKWELL FOREST PRESERVE

6.4-MILE LOOP	TRAIL	SCENERY RATING	
		HILL RATING	

Where have hundreds of high schoolers burned their quads? Where can you run knowing that 14,000 years ago a woolly mammoth tread the same ground? Not impressed? How about this: Where in Chicago can you find a bird's-eye view of the western suburbs that's 846 feet high? Read on.

ACCESS

About 30 miles west of the city. From Chicago, take I-290 to I-88 to I-355 (north) to Rte. 56 (Butterfield Rd.). Go 8.5 miles to the west entrance on the right side of the road, or stay on I-88 to Rte. 59 north and exit on Butterfield Rd., heading east, for 1.5 miles. There is plenty of parking available around Silver Lake.

COURSE

It's true; one of the most significant finds for DuPage County Forest Preserve's holdings is a skeleton of a woolly mammoth uncovered in 1977. That may pique your paleontological interests, but this course is great for a 10K race simulation with an added perk—one of the highest hills in DuPage County (albeit a landfill).

This is a nice, relatively flat multi-use course that's close to the Illinois Prairie Path (just on the other side of Butterfield Rd.) and is a section of the Regional Trail, which connects to Herrick Lake and the Danada Forest Preserves. Head left at the trailhead, but don't go to the far-left trail, which leads back to Butterfield Rd. Mt. Hoy and White Pines Pond will be on your right. You'll cross a bridge at just over 1 mile and cruise under a nice canopy of trees before reaching the only major road crossing, Mack Rd., at 1.7 miles. The second half of the trail consists mostly of marshes and meadows making an excellent birding area; look out into the fields for the nest boxes, which are intended to build up the bluebird population. From here, head left at the fork to do a

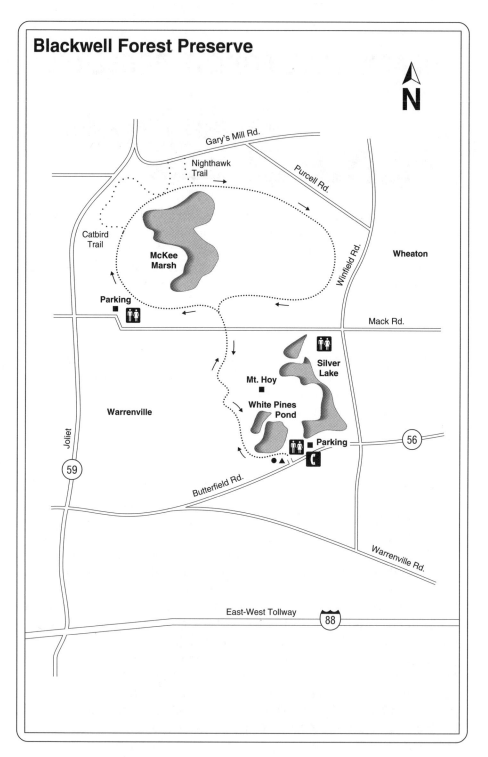

Blackwell Forest Preserve

N

Gary's Mill Rd.

Purcell Rd.

Nighthawk
Trail

Catbird
Trail

Winfield Rd.

Wheaton

McKee
Marsh

Parking

Mack Rd.

Silver
Lake

Mt. Hoy

White Pines
Pond

Warrenville

Parking

56

Joliet

59

Butterfield Rd.

Warrenville Rd.

East-West Tollway   88

small loop around McKee Marsh. At 2.5 miles, you have the opportunity to veer left to the Catbird Trail if you want to add on .8 mile; otherwise, keep right and you'll reach the 3-mile mark where the Catbird Trail re-emerges. Follow the main trail all the way back around McKee Marsh (4.3 miles); you'll cross Mack Rd. and follow the Regional Trail back to the trailhead. This might be a good point to do some charges up Mt. Hoy, as Olympian Jim Spivey recommends: "This is a great hill; we drive out there each week!" If you need to catch your breath at the top, you have the excuse of trying to spot a red-tailed hawk or bald eagle, both of which have been seen from this point.

FOOT NOTES

Silver Lake is stocked with bluegill, northern pike, and rainbow trout—a delight for anglers—and you can find a family camping area on the northern end, so it's ideal for a quick weekend getaway. For more information, contact the Forest Preserve District of DuPage County at 630-790-4900, or visit the Web site at **http://www.dupageforest.com**.

BUSSE WOODS

7.8-MILE LOOP	ROAD/TRAIL 👫 💧	SCENERY RATING	🌳🌳🌳
		HILL RATING	

Where in one day can you run, sail, fish, in-line skate, bike, and—check out a herd of elk? Yes, you read correctly! This 14-acre preserve is home to a small elk herd.

ACCESS

Three main entrances—Golf Rd., Higgins Rd., and Arlington Heights Rd.—each offer plenty of parking. The latter is the easiest if you're coming from the city. Take the Northwest Tollway (I-90) and exit at Arlington Heights Rd. South. Go a half mile to the entrance (just *before* Higgins Rd.). You can park in front of the restrooms.

COURSE

Officially known as the Ned Brown Forest Preserve, this northwest trail is conveniently sandwiched between Schaumburg, Rolling Meadows, Arlington Heights, and Elk Grove Village and is bisected by Higgins Rd. Meadows and plush forest blanket 3,700 acres of woodland.

You can pick up the paved path of this easy-to-follow flat loop to the right of the elk pasture. The route can be lengthened to 12-14 miles by running to the extension off Golf Rd. in the north end (not much shade here) and the extension on Biesterfield to the south. Unfortunately, the 100-foot hill was recently closed to the public. Busse Lake, one of the largest in Cook County, provides a focal point on the south side of Higgins; you'll know you're heading back to the elk pasture once you cross the newly constructed red bridge over Higgins Rd. You can make this a 20-miler by running 12 miles on the first loop and then 8 miles on the second loop.

On the first and third Thursdays in June through August you'll surely want to hook up with the Arlington Heights Trotters Running Club (see appendix, page 141) for their "beer" run. They meet at the Golf Rd. entrance around 6 P.M. (be sure to call in advance).

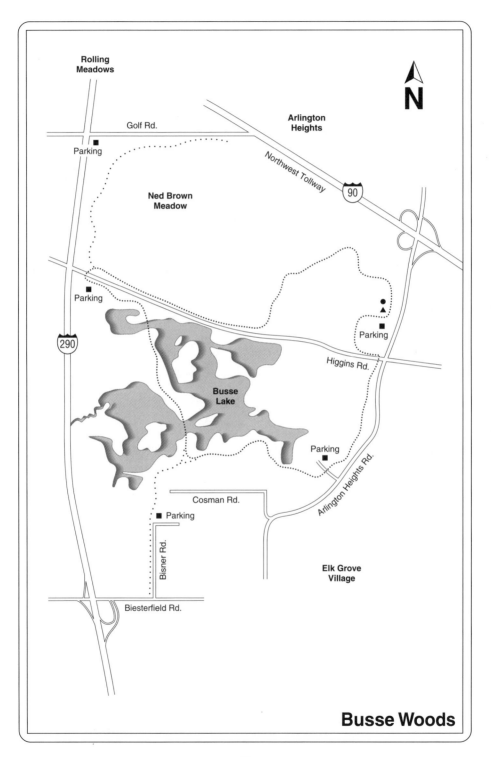

Rolling
Meadows

Arlington
Heights

N

Golf Rd.

Northwest Tollway

90

Parking

Ned Brown
Meadow

Parking

290

Parking

Higgins Rd.

Busse
Lake

Parking

Arlington Heights Rd.

Cosman Rd.

Parking

Bisner Rd.

Elk Grove
Village

Biesterfield Rd.

Busse Woods

TIPS

Summer months can be extremely crowded, with bikers and in-line skaters ignoring the 12 m.p.h. speed limit. Although the path is ideal for cross-country skiers and snowmobilers in the winter, local runners have come up with the "parking lot run," because the lots are plowed when temperatures plummet.

Two low-key races are held on this trail, if you're interested in a race where it doesn't take 10 minutes to reach the starting line. Check out the Summer Sizzler 5K and 10K; for information, call 708-771-1014. For the multisport athlete, a must for your race schedule is the Ridge 'n' Tie in November. For 10 years, this race draws a fun crowd of competitive teams who alternate running and mountain biking (kind of like leap frog where you can go into oxygen debt). This event is organized by the Runner's High in Arlington Heights; call 847-670-9255 for information.

FOX RIVER TRAIL MIDDLE SECTION (ST. CHARLES, GENEVA, AND BATAVIA)

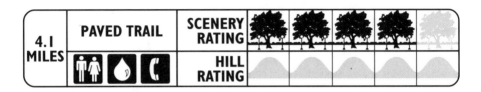

4.1 MILES	PAVED TRAIL	SCENERY RATING	
	🚻 💧 ☕	HILL RATING	

St. Charles had a number of Underground Railroad stations prior to the Civil War; Allan Pinkerton (world's first private detective) served as a deputy sheriff in Geneva; and Batavia was once known as the windmill manufacturing capital of the world. What does this have to do with running? Nothing, except you'll have plenty of time for mulling historical trivia as you explore this lengthy trail along the banks of the Fox River.

ACCESS

St. Charles (northern trailhead): From the Loop, take I-290 to I-88 (East-West Tollway) to Rte. 31 (north) to Rte. 64 (east) to Main St. Turn left on 2nd Ave. to North Ave. Parking is available at Pottawatomie Park.

Geneva (central trailhead): By Metra, take the Union Pacific West Line and head seven blocks west to the trail. For Metra information, call 847-836-7000, or visit **http://www.metrarail.com**.

Batavia (southern trailhead): From the Loop, take I-290 to I-88 (East-West Tollway). Exit at Farnsworth-North, which becomes Kirk Rd. Turn left at Fabyan Pkwy. and right on Rte. 25. Parking is available at Fabyan Forest Preserve. For more information, contact the Kane County Forest Preserve District at 630-232-2631, or visit the Web site at **http://www.co.kane.il.us/**.

COURSE

This is the most traveled and developed portion of a 36-mile, multi-purpose, paved trail, which extends south to Aurora and north to Crystal Lake (with future plans to extend to the state line). The route is

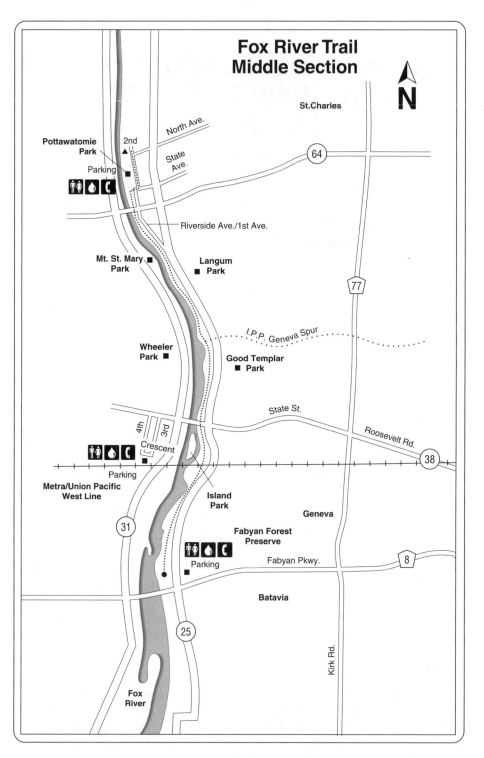

Fox River Trail
Middle Section

N

St.Charles

64

Pottawatomie
Park

2nd

North Ave.

State
Ave.

Parking

Riverside Ave./1st Ave.

Mt. St. Mary
Park

Langum
Park

77

I.P.P. Geneva Spur

Wheeler
Park

Good Templar
Park

State St.

4th

3rd

Crescent

Roosevelt Rd.

38

Parking

Metra/Union Pacific
West Line

Island
Park

Geneva

31

Fabyan Forest
Preserve

Parking

Fabyan Pkwy.

8

Batavia

25

Kirk Rd.

Fox
River

lauded by west suburban runners, including Illinois' first qualifier for the 2000 Olympic marathon trials, Ann Schaefers-Coles.

Start at East Fabyan Forest Preserve, which extends to both sides of the river, so there is a west side. Not only is this a beautiful spot for a picnic, but afterward you can visit the Villa Museum Japanese Garden and 68-foot Dutch Windmill, built in the 1850s. With a few dips and constant view of the river, you'll enjoy this gentle, winding course in all seasons—except during rainy weather, when flooding can be a problem. Although it's not plowed during winter months, enough runners frequent this section to forge a trail on the path. In Geneva, the path will guide you along the water's edge (north), where you'll see plenty of folks fishing and surely glimpse some great blue heron. Opportunities to add mileage or variety to your run include crossing to the west side. After you pass Main St. (Rte. 64), the path veers away from the water's edge, and you'll need to run on downtown sidewalks to reach the northern trailhead, Pottawatomie Park.

If you want to run away from your problems and are seeking solitude, the Batavia-Aurora section should satisfy your needs, and if you're looking for a hillier experience, you'll want to head north of St. Charles. Note: these areas are not heavily trafficked, so always use the buddy system.

FOOT NOTES

The Fox River Trail Runners are a fun group with an active membership. They host a variety of workouts in different locations, including 8 A.M. runs on Saturdays at the water treatment facility by Island Park, just north of East Fabyan Forest Preserve. Also, we would be remiss if we didn't mention another popular spot in Batavia, the Fermi National Accelerator Laboratory.

TIP

Check out the Illinois Prairie Path Southwest Branch (page 78), and you can hook up to the Northwest Branch via the Geneva Spur (see page 75).

GREAT WESTERN TRAIL (WESTERN BRANCH)

17.3 MILES	TRAIL	SCENERY RATING
	👫 💧 ☎	HILL RATING

Tired of urban running? Are your rural roots beckoning? This is the cure.

ACCESS

St. Charles (eastern trailhead): From the Loop, take I-290 to I-88 (East-West Tollway) to Rte. 31 (north) to Rte. 64 (west) to Randall Rd.; turn right. At the first light, turn left onto Dean St. Parking is on the left side of the road, and LeRoy Oakes Forest Preserve is across the street.

Sycamore (western trailhead): From the Loop, take I-290 to I-88 (East-West Tollway) to Rte. 47 (north) to Rte. 64 (west) to Old State Rd.

COURSE

This marked trail is a mixture of asphalt and crushed limestone with a few paved sections. Start at Horlock Hill Prairie. Named after St. Charles High School biology teacher Bob Horlock, it's one of the first prairie restoration projects in the county. This is a brief prologue to the most spectacular part of the trail—the first 3 miles, to the Burlington Rd. overpass bridge. During the summer, the trees form a dense canopy—a green ceiling of leaves—providing a cool passageway. The only close residential section is near the 4-mile stretch, but after that, except for an occasional house, it's farmland as far as the eye can see.

From Lily Lake through Sycamore, it's very flat, and the only company you'll find is an occasional runner or cyclist or the traffic from nearby Rte. 64. This should serve as a warning; with few people here, it's safer to run with someone. Near the 8-mile mark you'll be able to see a sign on Rte. 64 reading "Sycamore—11" (miles) and "Oregon—45." Okay, so it's not that western state, but at least you know you're

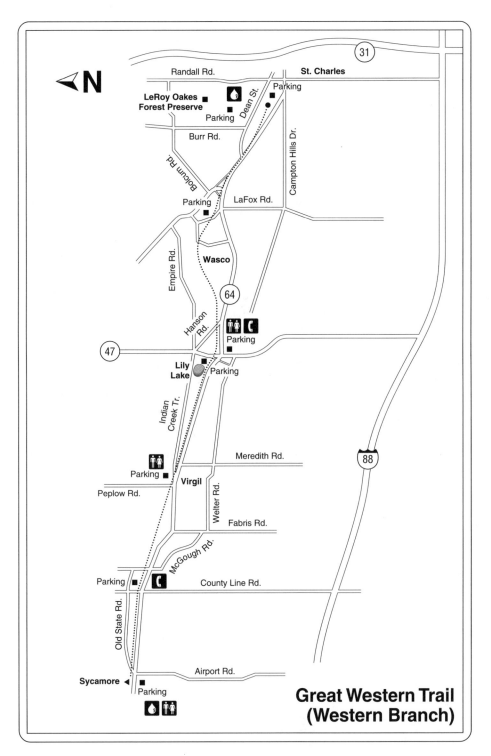

N

Randall Rd.

31

St. Charles

Parking

LeRoy Oakes
Forest Preserve

Dean St.

Parking

Parking

Burr Rd.

Campton Hills Dr.

Bolcum Rd.

Parking

LaFox Rd.

Empire Rd.

Wasco

64

Hanson Rd.

Parking

47

Lily
Lake

Parking

Indian Creek Tr.

Meredith Rd.

88

Parking

Virgil

Welter Rd.

Peplow Rd.

Fabris Rd.

McGough Rd.

Parking

County Line Rd.

Old State Rd.

Airport Rd.

Sycamore

Parking

Great Western Trail
(Western Branch)

heading in the right direction. The Sycamore trailhead is behind an old green building with old-fashioned gas pumps at Old State Rd., across from Brian Bemis Chevrolet.

FOOT NOTES

This trail is a popular training ground for stellar area athletes. The St. Charles High School girls' cross country team—Illinois AA 1998 champions—log in miles here. The Fox River Trail Runners (see appendix, page 141) meet on Wednesdays at 6 P.M. in the LeRoy Oakes Forest Preserve and cross over to the trail for long runs. They also host an out-and-back race, The Great Western 30K; for information, call 630-365-2252.

TIP

Workout for two. You need to squeeze in a long run to check out your shoes and test your endurance before the big marathon, but quality time with the special person in your life has been lacking. Here's an idea: the first section of the trail is rather romantic, so start out together for the first 3 miles or so, and then one can turn back, get the car, and meet the other at the Sycamore trailhead. Plan accordingly, and afterward you can enjoy the following options in this charming small town: antique shopping, the Polka Fest in June, or the Pumpkin Festival in October, which has a 10K race on the CARA race circuit. For more information, call the Sycamore Chamber of Commerce at 815-895-3456, or visit their Web site at **http://www.sycamorechamber.com**.

GREAT WESTERN TRAIL (EASTERN BRANCH)

11.5 MILES	TRAIL	SCENERY RATING					
		HILL RATING					

You won't find a ton of diversity or an exotic landscape, but this trail is perfect for the sun worshiper and anyone wanting to put in some solid distance training—just remember to bring along water.

ACCESS

Villa Park trailhead: From the city, take I-290 to St. Charles Rd. West. At Villa Ave., turn left just beyond Wildwood St. The 0-mile marker is near Pioneer Garden & Feed. There are several access roads that have parking near the path in Villa Park, Lombard, Carol Stream, and Winfield.

COURSE

Except for a few overpass inclines, this is a straight, smooth, crushed-limestone trail. A key feature is its accessibility to the Illinois Prairie Path (I.P.P.) Main Stem (see page 72), just south of Villa Park, and the I.P.P. Northwest Branch (see page 75), just west of Prince Crossing Rd. If you're deciding between the I.P.P and this trail, here are a couple of reasons to go for the Great Western: 1) the fact that there are fewer trees means less maintenance and faster-melting snow in winter, and 2) the higher ground spells better drainage—key during the early spring.

Because of construction at the time of this writing, one spot had confusing signage. At approximately 1.5 miles, you cross St. Charles Rd. and the sign says to follow the arrow straight ahead to Grace St. and take the sidewalk. Well, the sidewalk is straight ahead, but you need to turn right to Grace St., which is at the St. Charles Rd.–Parkside St.–Grace St. intersection. Once you're here, there's no sign. Turn right and cross the railroad tracks to pick up the trail about 100 feet further. Lombard street crossings impressively note first aid and fire station directions.

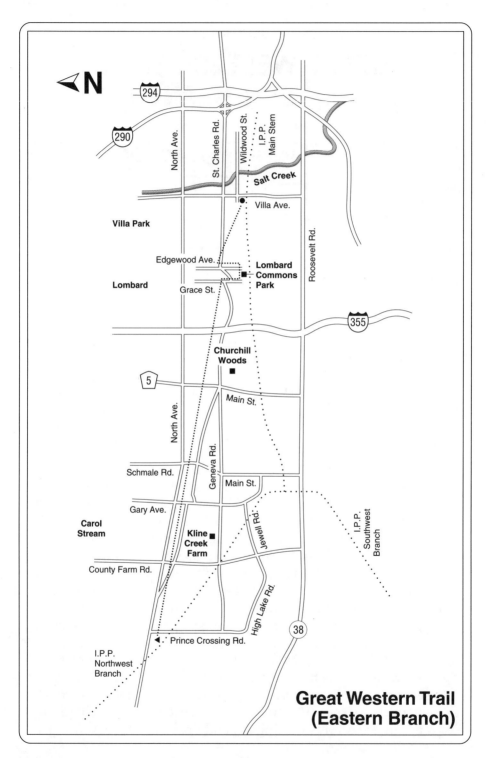

**Great Western Trail
(Eastern Branch)**

After 3.5 miles, you'll cross the I-355 overpass. Churchill Woods Forest Preserve is to the south, houses are fewer, and in the summer the main sound you'll hear is the gentle hum of cicadas blending with the hum from the numerous high-tension wires lining the path. At 7.5 miles, you'll pass a small fenced site, St. Stephen Cemetery, where German pioneers from the mid-1800s are buried. Past County Farm Rd., at approximately 9.5 miles, is a sign leading to Timber Ridge trail and Kline Creek Farm, an authentic 1890s working farm that offers educational programs such as making apple butter. For more information, call 630-876-5900, or visit **www.dupageforest.com**. Although this trail dead-ends at the I.P.P. Northwest Branch intersection (see page 75), you can pick up the western branch just north of St. Charles (see page 66).

As always, use caution at busy street crossings, and try not to run alone. Restroom and water opportunities are pretty much nil; you can find a few spots parallel to the path (at 4.2 miles, near the baseball diamonds/soccer fields; at 7 miles, at the Schmale Rd. crossing gas station; and at 8 miles, at the Gary Ave. crossing). The Barn Garden Center has a soda machine visible from the path and a pay phone.

TIP

One day I heard strains of Danny & the Juniors singing "Rock 'n roll is here to stay, it will never die . . . " Although I agree with the lyrics, I thought I was hallucinating, so I stopped and discovered Augustino's Rock 'n Roll Deli (246 Schmale Rd.). This 50s-themed deli regularly pipes out music and offers an array of sandwiches and pizza.

ILLINOIS PRAIRIE PATH MAIN STEM (WHEATON TO ELMHURST)

10.5 MILES	ROAD	SCENERY RATING	🌳 🌳 🌳
	🚻 💧 ☎	HILL RATING	⌃⌃⌃⌃⌃

What a treat! One of the first rails-to-trails paths in the country, this 61-mile-long multi-use trail connects Cook, DuPage, and Kane counties. May Theilgaard Watts, an environmentalist who loved hiking, is the person to thank for spearheading this trail. In 1963, she wrote to the *Chicago Tribune,* proposing to convert the abandoned Chicago, Aurora, and Elgin right-of-ways into a trail. This 10-foot-wide trail is to the western suburbs what the lakefront is to city dwellers. The path is maintained today by dedicated volunteers.

ACCESS

Wheaton trailhead: From the city, take I-290 to I-88 to I-355 (north) to Rte. 38 (Roosevelt Rd.). At Carlton St., turn right and go three blocks to Liberty St. (Founders Park). By Metra, take the Union Pacific West line to Front/West St. (approximately three blocks east of the trailhead).

    Elmhurst trailhead: From the city (by car), take I-290 to St. Charles Rd. West. At York Rd. turn left to the trailhead by Seminole Ave. By Metra, take the Union Pacific West line to York/1st Ave., run south on Cottage Hill Ave. about three-quarters of a mile to the path. You can usually find both free and metered parking near the path, especially in Wheaton, Glen Ellyn, Lombard, and Villa Park.

COURSE

For the purposes of this guide and for continuity, these entries start where all trails converge at the Wheaton trailhead; but, of course, you don't have to start here—this really is an easy-access trail.

    At the 0-mile marker at Liberty St. head east, parallel to the tracks, picking up the trail on Main St. Miles 1 through 4.5 pass through Wheaton and Glen Ellyn, where scenery varies from grassy lands to

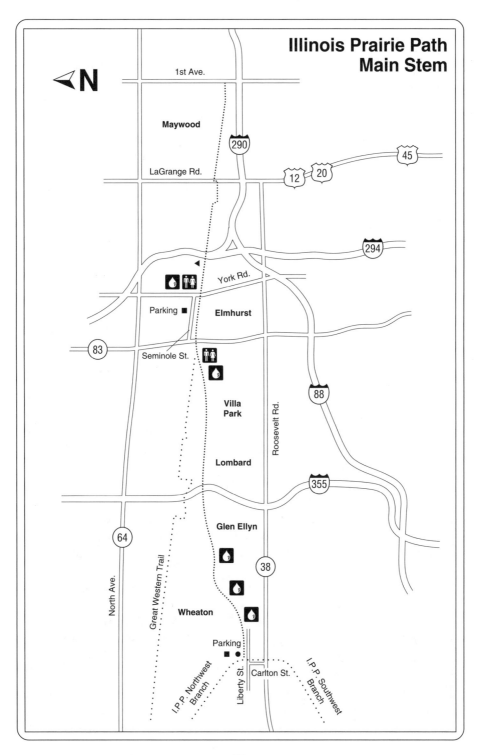

heavily wooded stretches hiding nearby houses; occasionally a shopping district pops up. At 4.5 miles, you'll find the bridge over I-355 provides a good incline and descent. A few "you are here" maps assist you along the way, and as always buddy up—especially in the evening—even in the well-lit Elmhurst and Villa Park sections. The Villa Park visitor's center has restrooms and water, and there's a portable toilet near York Rd. in Elmhurst (near the farmer's market). Street crossings are inevitable, but the streets are usually not heavily trafficked and several crossing signs are marked with the street names (a very helpful feature!). At the 8.5-mile mark the path joins the Great Western Trail (East) (see page 69), and a railroad crossing by Pioneer Park is at 9.2 miles.

In Elmhurst, check out the Interpretive Garden at Berkley St. filled with labeled plants. Winter running can be a challenge, but a poem by J. Pracht on the map board near this section sums it up: "Winter Prairie—Rugged, Empty, Peaceful, Open, Silent, yet Everlasting." In any season, this trail provides everlasting enjoyment for all who frequent it and a pleasant reminder of our heritage—the wavy seas of grasslands that awed the first Illinois settlers.

SPIVEY'S SEAL OF APPROVAL

Jim Spivey competed for the U.S. Olympic Track and Field Team in 1984, 1992, and 1996. He has several Chicago connections. In addition to living in Glen Ellyn, he's currently the head coach for the University of Chicago men's and women's track and field and cross country teams. Spivey recommends the Illinois Prairie Path for its mile markers and its straight, flat course. As one of America's best, we all know he's got talent and speed (PRs include 3:31:01 for 1500 meters and 3:49:80 for the mile), but he has an added advantage for getting to the path, "I can get there in 2 minutes and 7 seconds from my house." Bob Richards, editor of *Chicago's Amateur Athlete* and Villa Park resident, regularly trains here, too. "It's great for long-time runners, and the forgiving surface gives my body some needed shock-absorption, enabling me to get in longer runs." He adds, "Some sections will protect you from the heat in the summer and the extreme cold in the winter." His favorite after-a-good-run breakfast spot is Uncle Andy's Restaurant (621 E. St. Charles Rd., just three blocks north of the path in Villa Park. Phone: 630-941-7262).

ILLINOIS PRAIRIE PATH NORTHWEST BRANCH (WHEATON TO ELGIN)

11.5 MILES	ROAD	SCENERY RATING					
		HILL RATING					

In Wheaton, the historic 1906 bridge beckons runners to cross its planks to a spectacular journey filled with marshes, forest preserves and—what's that? The sound of a hunting horn? Riders geared up in red coats, breeches, and black boots galloping by? Hounds baying in the distance? Guess what; you're probably near Pratt's Wayne Woods.

ACCESS

Wheaton trailhead: If you're driving from the city, take I-290 to I-88 to I-355 (north) to Rte. 38 (Roosevelt Rd.). At Carlton St., turn right and go three blocks to Liberty St. (Founders Park). By Metra, take the Union Pacific West line to Front/West St. (approximately three blocks east of the trailhead).

Elgin trailhead: From the city, take I-94 north to I-90 to Rte. 25 (south) to Chicago St. and Raymond St., where you can park in the public lots. By Metra, take the Milwaukee District West line to Elgin (although not too close to the path, it's close to the Fox River trail, which links to the path just north of Raymond St.).

Geneva Spur trailhead: From the city, take I-290 to I-88 to I-355 (north) to Rte. 38 (Roosevelt Rd.) and head north to the County Farm and Geneva Rd. intersection. For more information, call the CTA/RTA at 773-836-7000, or check the Web site at **http://www.metrarail.com**.

COURSE

From the Wheaton trailhead over the bridge, your first attraction is Lincoln Marsh. (An important source for wildlife, marshes help with flood control and water quality. In fact, an educational sign notes

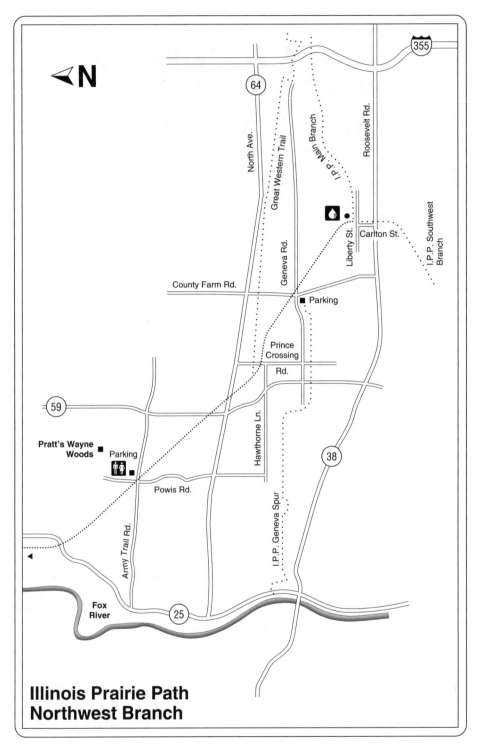

**Illinois Prairie Path
Northwest Branch**

there's enough land for storm water to fill 7,000 swimming pools.) Adhere to the pedestrian crossing signs at County Farm and Geneva Rds., a busy intersection at 2.5 miles where you'll find a map on the north side directing you onward or off to the Geneva Spur or Timber Ridge trail (which connects to the Great Western Trail). The next stretch through the Timber Ridge Forest Preserve, 2.5 to 5 miles, is pretty flat and rather isolated except for a few street crossings that remind you residential areas are nearby. The 5 to 6 mile portion has some industrial areas, and there are two bridge crossings: one at 5.8 miles (Rte. 64), and the other at 6.5 miles (Rte. 59).

Pratt's Wayne Woods highlights the second half of the route, a tranquil setting with savannas, bur and white oak trees, colorful wildflowers, and a vast area of wetlands (home to waterfowl like the egret, the endangered sandhill crane, and beavers). If your run is interrupted by a hunting horn, don't worry; it's just members of Wayne DuPage Hunt Club holding an English-style fox hunt (animal lovers need not fret; a scented rag substitutes for a live fox). At 9 miles, you can stop at the Wayne Country Store, where you can find restrooms and phone. This section of the I.P.P. continues north into Elgin and connects, at approximately 13.8 miles, with the Fox River Trail (see page 63).

ILLINOIS PRAIRIE PATH
SOUTHWEST BRANCH
(WHEATON TO AURORA)

12.5 MILES	ROAD 👫 💧 📞	SCENERY RATING	🌳🌳🌳
		HILL RATING	

Aurora isn't just home to *Saturday Night Live's* Wayne and Garth or robo-babes, it's the southwest cornerstone linking the Illinois Prairie Path to the Fox River Trail, with the bonus of the Batavia Spur. All of these options totally rock!

ACCESS

Wheaton trailhead: If you are driving from the city, take I-290 to I-88 to I-355 (north) to Rte. 38 (Roosevelt Rd.). At Carlton St., turn right and go three blocks to Liberty St. (Founders Park). By Metra, take the Union Pacific West line to Front/West St. (approximately three blocks east of the trailhead).

Aurora trailhead: Just off Illinois Ave., park at McCullough Park on the west side of the Fox River and pick up the trail on the east side of the river. By Metra, take the Burlington Northern line. Park in the commuter lot on the east side of Rte. 25.

Batavia Spur trailhead: From I-88, take Rte. 77 (Farnsworth Ave.) to Bilter Rd. The trailhead can also be accessed at Glenwood Park Forest Preserve in Batavia, on the west side of Rte. 25.

COURSE

To start, run back out Carlton St. and cross Roosevelt Rd. at the stoplight, where you can see the trail's flat, cushioned surface. This section has a smorgasbord of options: you can link to different paths, like the Batavia Spur and the Fox River Trail (see page 63), and access points are plenty. You can run with the CARA marathon training group, which meets in Warrenville on Saturdays between 7:00 and 7:30 A.M. (see

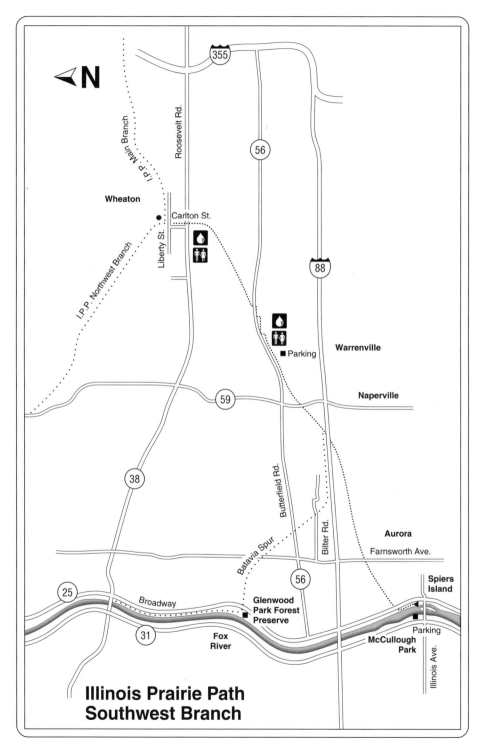

Illinois Prairie Path Southwest Branch

page 141). Warrenville is a favored spot on this trail (with restrooms and water stops). In 1838, founding father "Colonel" Julius Morton Warren built a tavern that was a popular stagecoach stop; he'd be proud to know the tradition continues—for foot travelers, that is.

Be sure to carry water; hot summer days can leave you scorched, especially along the 7- to 10-mile stretch filled with cornfields and little shade. Winter running here can also be difficult (the snow is not plowed), but if you're so inclined, it's sure to build character.

TIP

In Warrenville, just west of Winfield Dr., you can cross over to the Blackwell Forest Preserve trail (see page 57).

OAK PARK

5- & 8-MILE LOOPS	ROAD	SCENERY RATING				
		HILL RATING				

A must for any architecture lover! Oak Park has the world's largest collection of Frank Lloyd Wright-designed buildings and houses. For more information, contact the Oak Park Visitor's Center at 158 Forest Ave., 708-524-7472, or check out this Web site: **http://www.oprf.com/ tourism/index.html**.

ACCESS

Just 10 miles west of the Loop. By car: take I-290 to Austin Blvd. (the exit is in the *left* lane). Turn right and go a little over a mile to Lake St.; turn left to East St. There's plenty of street parking. By CTA, take the Green line to Lake St./Ridgeland or Lake St./Oak Park; East St. is between these stops.

COURSE

Want an introduction to these courses and don't feel like running alone? Join the Oak Park Runners Club on Mondays at 6:30 P.M. For more information, see page 142.

5-mile loop: From the Oak Park/River Forest High School (where Hemingway graduated and wrote for the school paper) on the corner of Lake and East Sts., head north up Scoville Rd., which turns into Fair Oaks after Chicago Ave. At Le Moyne, take a quick jog right to Austin and back to Belleforte. Cut left through Lindberg Park and head south on Forest St. Arguably the best-looking street in Oak Park, it showcases much of Wright's work. His style is exemplified by the use of interior light and open spaces. At the north end of the 400 block, the Planter House has fabulous flower beds in the front sidewalk, and the Nathan G. Moore House (English Tudor style) has wonderful lines. At the south end, one of my favorites is the Frank Thomas house, the first prairie-style house.

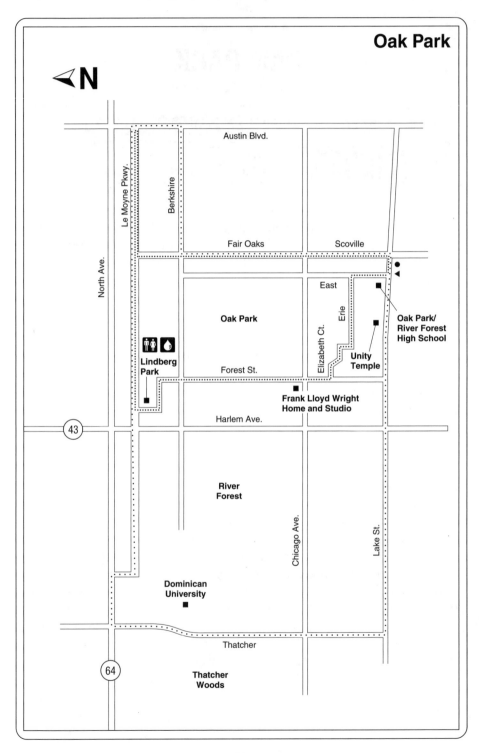

Oak Park

8-mile loop: Follow the 5-mile course up Scoville Rd./Fair Oaks, turning right at Berkshire. For a relatively flat course, there's a slight incline before Ridgeland. At Austin, you'll need to hop on the sidewalk for just a quarter mile before heading left onto Le Moyne. A good halfway stop for water and restrooms is Lindberg Park on the corner of Le Moyne and Marion, and then you cross the busiest street, Harlem. Continue to the end of Le Moyne, make a slight right turn to North Ave., and jump back onto the sidewalk to Thatcher. Turn left and take this past Dominican University (formerly Rosary College), a beautiful stretch next to the Thatcher Woods. At Lake St. turn left, and be alert for shoppers and Wright's Unity Temple on Kenilworth, a lasting legacy of beauty and serenity.

FOOT NOTES

An overnight parking ban on most Oak Park residential streets makes them inviting to runners; however, they're dark, so wear proper reflective wear, be alert to oncoming traffic, and hop onto the sidewalk when appropriate.

SEE JANE RUN. TRY THE "WRIGHT" RUN.

If you don't recognize the name Jane Murphy, you'll certainly recognize her face—she was featured on full-page Nike ads in *Chicago's Amateur Athlete* and *Windy City Sports*. With a 2:44 PR, this Olympic marathon trials qualifier (1988 and 1996) and Trinity High School/DePaul University graduate trains through these canopy-covered streets regularly and highly recommends the Frank Lloyd Wright Run. "It's not a fast course," says the veteran champ, noting the many turns; "however, you can turn the race into a *real* workout if you do the 'Double Race' and run both the 5K and 10K." With a 45-minute difference in starting times, you can use each distance as either a warm-up or a cooldown. For information, call 708-383-0002.

THE SOUTH

1. I & M Canal State Trail (Eastern Section)
2. Indiana Dunes
3. Old Plank Road
4. Palos Hills Forest Preserve
5. Sag Valley Forest Preserve
6. Salt Creek Trail (Brookfield Zoo)
7. Waterfall Glen

Skip the traffic jams to Wisconsin's Door County. If you must experience the change in seasons, just check out any of these stellar South Side runs. They're great during all seasons, but especially in the fall, when these trails explode with crimson, gold, and bronze colors drizzling throughout the surrounding woods and prairies. The colors offer a stunning backdrop to some of the most exciting and challenging courses in this guide.

Let's start with the easier and work up to some rigorous trails. The Old Plank Road and Salt Creek trails offer paved paths that link to fun destinations for the whole family. After that, as the song says, "If you ever plan to motor west (or in this case, southwest)/travel my way/take the highway that's the best/get your kicks on Route 66/It winds from Chicago to . . ." Channahon, for the I & M Canal State Trail. Believe me, you'll appreciate my timely tip—it's flat, long, and hip. Waterfall Glen's winding, rolling path is a great escape with a few surprises. Palos Hills Forest Preserve and its neighboring Sag Valley Forest Preserve raise the level of difficulty. If you love running cross country, you'll make the trip down here often.

Now, the Indiana Dunes aren't in Illinois, but they're closer than many of the western entries if you don't try to get there during rush hour. Dune testimonials poured in from many runners; my favorite is

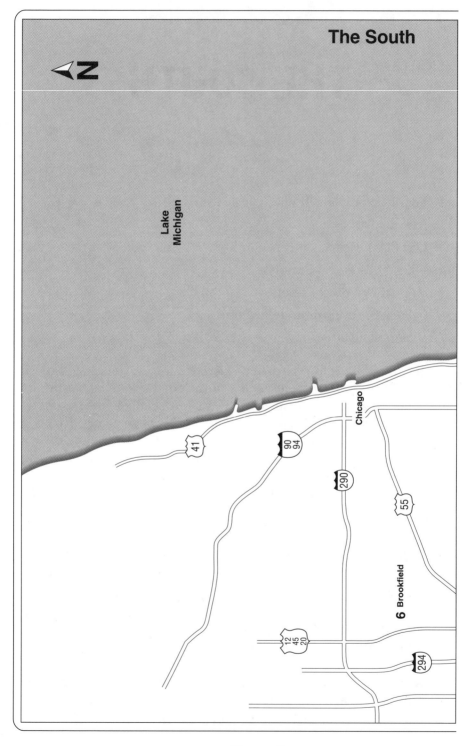

N

Lake
Michigan

41

90
94

290

55

Chicago

6 Brookfield

12
45
20

294

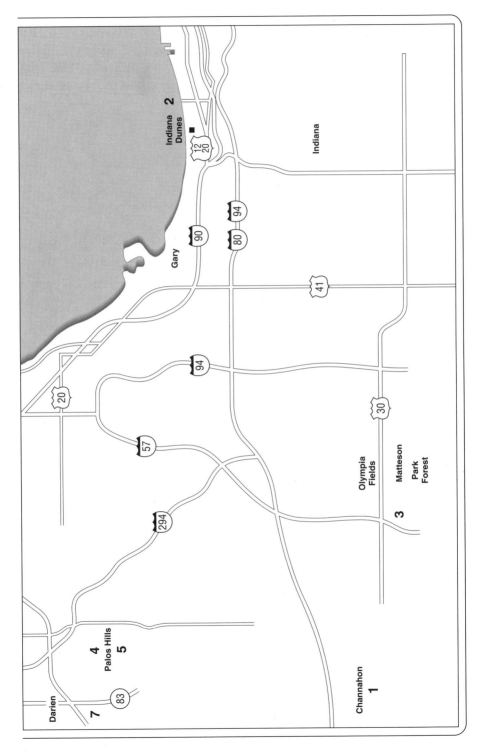

Indiana Dunes **2**

Indiana

Gary

94

90

80

41

94

20

30

57

294

Olympia Fields

Matteson

Park Forest

3

Palos Hills

4

5

83

Darien

7

Channahon

1

from Dave Macknick: "If I found out I only had one week to live, I'd want to run the Indiana Dunes twice." If you've never experienced the exhilaration and challenge of trying to run through soft sand one minute and entering a shrouded forest the next, you must add these trails to your weekend workout schedule.

I & M CANAL STATE TRAIL
(EASTERN SECTION)

14.8 MILES	DIRT TRAIL	SCENERY RATING	
	🚻 💧 ☎	HILL RATING	

I & M stands for Illinois and Michigan; for runners, it could also mean Incredible and Marvelous.

ACCESS

About 50 miles from the city. By car, take I-55 west to Rte 6., turn right at Exit 248, go through town 2.5 miles to Canal St., then turn left and go a half mile to the Channahon access entrance (on the right). Parking, restrooms, and phone are available. For maps and more information, call the I & M Canal Information Center at 815-942-0796.

COURSE

There's something almost spiritual about this trail; maybe it's because the very flat course allows you a chance to run "in the zone" with minimal interruptions. Still undiscovered by many runners, this packed gravel trail continues for 51 miles, from Channahon to LaSalle. (Note: not to be confused with the popular I & M Canal bicycle trail near Palos Hills.)

We cover the first 14.8 miles of the trail. At the Channahon trailhead, you'll see the only mileage sign: McKinley Woods 2.8 miles, Dresden Access 5.8 miles, Aux Sable 8.1 miles, and Gebhard Woods 14.8 miles. Throughout this run you're sure to see many joys of nature: white-tail deer, turtles sunning themselves, and squirrels scampering about in the mulberry and cottonwood trees.

The first 5 miles remind me of the harmony I feel when kayaking, because there's water that not only borders the path but is at the same level. An old red barn marks the Dresden Access area, and across the water you can see a tavern that was once a stagecoach stop. At the

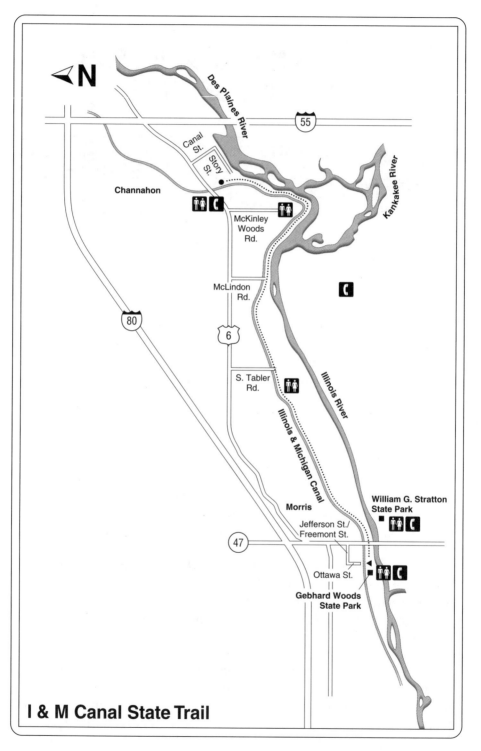

I & M Canal State Trail

Aux Sable stop, check out an engineering feat at lock #8, "the only place where a lock and aqueduct occur close together."

You'll know you're coming to the William G. Stratton State Park when you see the boat launching area beneath the bridge over the Illinois River.

TIP

This towpath is also the home course for the National Heritage Corridor 25K (which starts at Channahon trailhead), a perfect preparatory long-distance race before your fall marathon. For more information, call 815-744-5768.

INDIANA DUNES

VARI-OUS MILE-AGE	TRAIL	SCENERY RATING	
		HILL RATING	

Shhhh . . . let me entice you with one of the best-kept secrets among Chicagoland trail runners: the Indiana Dunes. This network of challenging and stunning trails along dunes, wetlands, marshes, and prairies offers spectacular views of Lake Michigan and is a perfect escape from the city. Hal Higdon, senior editor of *Runner's World*, says, "This is one of the best running areas—if not the best—in America."

ACCESS

Just 50 miles from the Loop. By car, take I-90/I-94 south to the Indiana Tollway/Skyway (I-90 south) to Rte. 12-20 east at Exit 17. This splits almost immediately; follow Rte. 12 (Dunes Hwy.) east.

Indiana Dunes State Park—*Wilson Shelter trailhead:* On Rte. 12 (Dunes Hwy.) after Midwest & Bethlehem Steel, follow signs for the state park at Rte. 49, approximately 10 miles after you get on Rte. 12. Entrance fee is $2 for Indiana residents and $5 for Illinois residents. Past the gate, turn right and follow the signs to Wilson Shelter (about a mile). For more information, call 219-926-1952.

National Lakeshore trailheads—*Cowles Bog Trail:* Go east on Rte. 12 (before Rte. 49) to Mineral Springs Rd. *Kemil Beach:* Continue east on Rte. 12 to the Kemil Rd./E. State Park Rd. intersection. Turn left on E. State Park Rd. Follow one mile to the parking lot (on the right) before the beach. Note: The Dorothy Buell Memorial Visitor Center on Kemil Rd. (south side of Rte. 12) provides detailed maps and brochures. For information, call 219-926-7561, or go to **http://www.nps.gov/indu/**.

By Metra, take the South Shore line from Randolph St. to Dune Park or Beverly Shores. For information, call the CTA/RTA at 773-836-7000 or visit **http://www.metrarail.com**.

COURSES

Note: this is only a sampling to get you started. I'm sure you'll be hooked and will make multiple trips to explore the 25 miles of shoreline

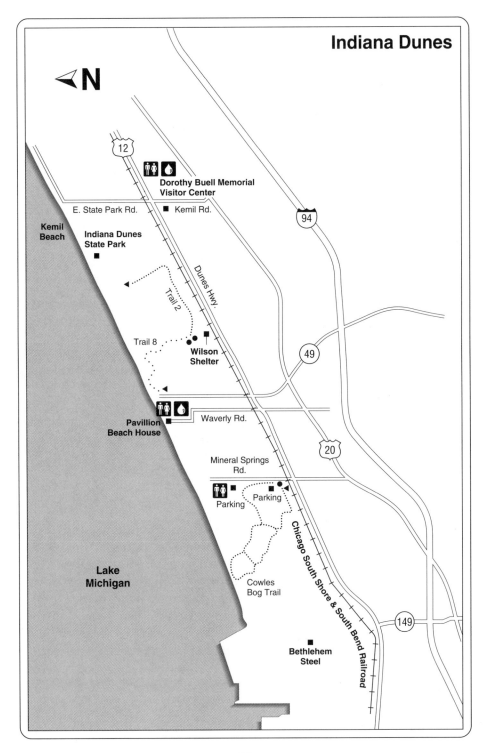

Indiana Dunes

N

12

94

Dorothy Buell Memorial
Visitor Center

E. State Park Rd.   Kemil Rd.

Kemil
Beach

Indiana Dunes
State Park

Dunes Hwy.

Trail 2

Trail 8

Wilson
Shelter

49

Pavillion
Beach House

Waverly Rd.

20

Mineral Springs
Rd.

Parking   Parking

Cowles
Bog Trail

Lake
Michigan

Chicago South Shore & South Bend Railroad

149

Bethlehem
Steel

surrounded by over 15,000 acres (2,000 acres in the state park). You'll encounter trails of soft sand and hilly blowouts sure to make you yell "Cowabunga!" You'll run in thick forests and come out along ridges where you'll see glimmering Lake Michigan on one side and never-ending tree-tops on the other. Like me, you'll probably wonder, Am I really in Indiana?

INDIANA DUNES STATE PARK TRAILS—WILSON SHELTER TRAILHEAD

Trail #2: 3 miles. Pick this up at the Wilson picnic grounds. Perfect for a relaxed out-and-back run that follows the marsh and heads across a boardwalk, where it links to Trails #9 and #10.

Trail #8: 1.5 miles. *Extremely* challenging. Start by the huge boulder, follow the markers across the boardwalk, and bam! you've got your first uphill through deep, soft sand, and it doesn't stop with just one: after Mt. Jackson (elev. 176 feet), there's Mt. Holden (elev. 184 feet) and then Mt. Tom (elev. 192 feet). This trail leads to the pavilion and beach house and links to several other trails.

INDIANA DUNES NATIONAL LAKESHORE TRAILS

Cowles Bog Trail: 4.6 miles. A designated National Nature Landmark named after University of Chicago professor and botany chair Henry Cowles. Teeming with diverse plant life, the Indiana Dunes ranks seventh among national parks in native plant diversity.

Kemil Beach: Various trails. Every Sunday at 8 A.M. a group of runners meet in the parking lot here for various trail runs. This is an excellent opportunity to hook up with those familiar with the ins and outs of these trails.

FOOT NOTES

Al Mussman, race director of the now-defunct "underground" Zoy Run (this race grew via word of mouth from 37 entrants to 800 in 1997 before the state park put the kibosh on it), recommends coming to the Dunes even for winter running: "The frozen, wet sand can be rough on the ankles, but the woods are warmer and shelter you from the wind." Finally, if you listen closely, you're supposed to be able to hear the "singing sands" of the dunes from the water's edge. A clear, ringing sound is caused by a fusion of moisture, quartz crystals, sea pressure, and friction from your feet.

TIP

During the summer months, wear a baseball cap to keep deer flies at bay.

OLD PLANK ROAD

12 MILES	ROAD	SCENERY RATING					
		HILL RATING					

Currently, this east-west route links Park Forest, Matteson, Rich Township, Frankfort, and the Will County Forest Preserve District. Future plans include a link to Joliet.

ACCESS

Eastern trailhead: From the city, take I-94 south to I-57, then exit (east) on Rte. 30 (Lincoln Hwy.) and go a half mile to the start at Western Ave., just south of Hickory Ln. A good spot for parking is on Main St., just south of 214th St. From the Loop, take the Metra Electric at Michigan Ave. (between S. Water and Randolph Sts.) to Matteson (215th and Main Sts.).

Western trailhead: From the city, take I-94 south to I-57, then to I-80 (west) to Rte. 45. Go south to Rte. 30 (Lincoln Hwy.), past Wolf Rd., to Hickory Creek Junction.

COURSE

This 10-foot-wide asphalt trail, shared by bikers and runners, now follows the former Penn Central Railroad right-of-way in Will and Cook counties and is slated to link up with the I & M Canal State Trail (see page 89). The eastern trailhead is just north of the Park Forest Scenic 10-Mile course (see page 136) and south of the Heart and Sole 10K course (see page 123). Mile markers are an asset for documenting your logbook entries on this fairly flat and straight-as-an-arrow trail.

Key spots include scenic prairie lands, especially along the Dewey Helmick Nature Preserve (past Central Ave.), where big bluestem grass and heart-leaved aster are among the hundreds of types of flora. Near Kean Ave./Rte. 45 is a quaint little town, Frankfort, with an ornate iron sign reading *Plank Road Trail*. This is a wonderful spot. Get some water and browse around the shops; the Trolley Barn (11 S. White St.) is a popular antique marketplace (and restroom stop). Further west

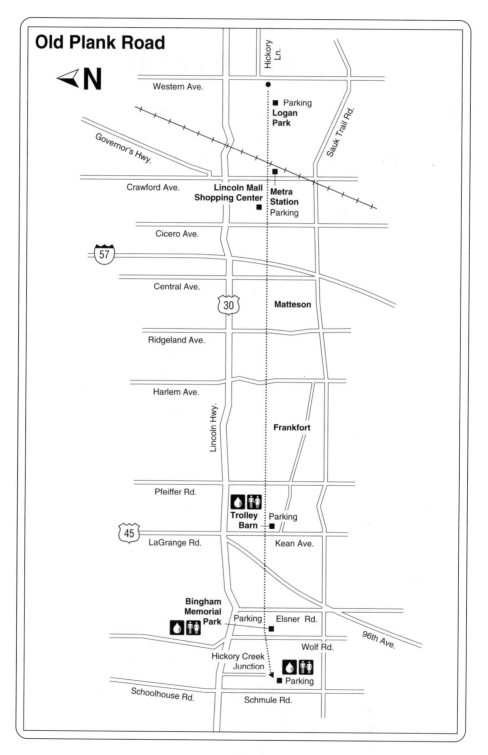

Old Plank Road

◀ **N**

Western Ave.

Hickory Ln.

Governor's Hwy.

Sauk Trail Rd.

■ Parking
Logan Park

Crawford Ave.

Lincoln Mall Shopping Center

Metra Station
Parking

Cicero Ave.

57

Central Ave.

30 **Matteson**

Ridgeland Ave.

Lincoln Hwy.

Harlem Ave.

Frankfort

Pfeiffer Rd.

Trolley Barn Parking

45

LaGrange Rd. Kean Ave.

Bingham Memorial Park

Parking Elsner Rd.

96th Ave.

Wolf Rd.

Hickory Creek Junction

Parking

Schoolhouse Rd. Schmule Rd.

is the Michele Bingham Memorial Park with softball and soccer fields and restroom facilities. A slight curve in the path as you cross a pedestrian bridge over Rte. 45 signals the western trailhead, Hickory Creek Junction—a pleasant picnic area with year-round restrooms/water. Already the trail has been extended to Cedar Rd. in New Lenox. Like most trails, this one can be barren in the winter months (you shouldn't run alone) and icy in the early spring.

FOOT NOTES

For more information on the Old Plank Road trail in Matteson, call 708-283-4900 or contact the Forest Preserve District of Will County at 815-727-8700.

TIPS

Frankfort's Fall Festival, which is usually held around Labor Day, has fun activities for the whole family. If you've been training hard for that 10K race and put in the necessary miles, you must reward yourself with a visit to the Creamery (459 W. Nebraska St., near Rte. 45), open mid-March through October. Try one of their yummy turtle sundaes!

PALOS HILLS FOREST PRESERVE

Known as *the* spot for trails, runners looking for a challenge will surely find it here among the 14,000 acres of Cook County's largest forest preserve. Challenge yourself on this maze of packed dirt trails, and be prepared to tackle some rugged terrain. Take the whole family for an educational outing at the Little Red Schoolhouse, built in 1886, for just one of many outdoor activities available.

ACCESS

Just 20 miles southwest of the Loop. By car, take I-90/I-94 south to I-55 (toward St. Louis), and exit at LaGrange Rd. South (Rte. 45, 12, 20). Continue to 95th St. and head west, following the curve around Maple Lake (take care at the fork; it's a blind corner). Park at Pulaski Woods Grove #1, where you can find a water pump and restroom.

COURSE

There are many entry points; here are two popular runs.

  1. Bullfrog Lake 3-mile loop (well, almost; 2.92 miles). Head straight down the slope (with the lake to your right). Follow the trail to the right for a tough rollercoaster run. At 1.5 miles, you can hear the cars passing on the highway below the steep incline. At 2.1 miles, take a sharp right turn. The next stretch is confusing, but keep right past two outhouses; Maple Lake is across the road to the left. Run along the single-track perimeter of the Maple Lake Woods #3 until you come upon Bullfrog Lake and see this sign: "Keeper bass must be 14 inches." Head left up the hill to the parking lot.

  2. For a 10-mile loop, head down the same slope, but pick up the main path (left) and head east to the Little Red Schoolhouse at the 1-mile mark. At 2 miles, you'll come to your first fork. Keep going straight; shortly you'll come upon another fork (left) as you pass

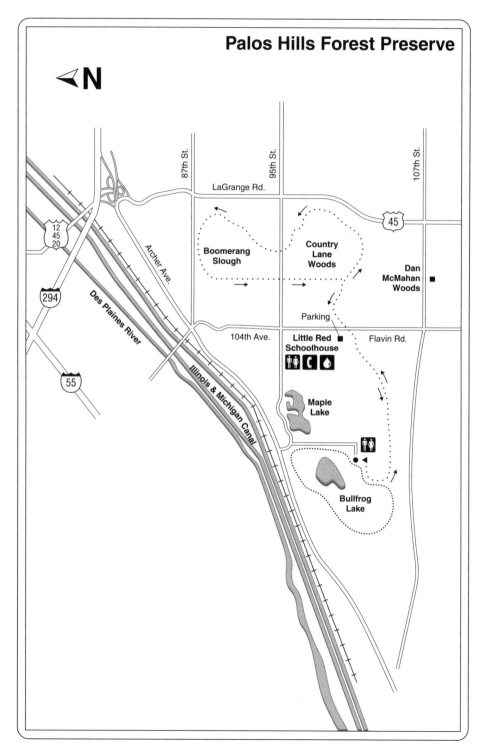

Palos Hills Forest Preserve

N

87th St.

95th St.

107th St.

LaGrange Rd.

45

12
45
20

Archer Ave.

294

Des Plaines River

Boomerang Slough

Country Lane Woods

Dan McMahan Woods

Parking

104th Ave.

Little Red Schoolhouse

Flavin Rd.

Illinois & Michigan Canal

55

Maple Lake

Bullfrog Lake

through the Country Lane Woods and Buttonbush Slough, heading north toward the Boomerang Slough at 4.3 miles. Keep to the left; you'll come to a straightaway and head directly south. At 7 miles, you'll turn right and head back to the schoolhouse (7.8 miles) and the parking lot overlooking Bullfrog Lake.

If you're adventurous, there are plenty of single tracks where you can blaze your own trails; just be aware of the signage and be respectful of closed trails (there has been some tension recently between park officials and bicyclists on this issue).

For more information, call the Cook County Forest Preserve/Palos Division Headquarters at 708-839-5617.

SHOPPING FOR HILLS?

Marshall Field may have had shoppers in mind when he coined his famous motto, "Give the lady what she wants," but training at Palos Hills gives Olympic hopeful Mary Knisely (1986 U.S. outdoor champion in the 3,000 meters and a 2:35:16 marathon PR) exactly what *she* wants: plenty of wide trails and a reprieve from the hot summer sun. "The shade takes a little bit out of the heat factor, which helps you recover a lot faster." When asked to describe Palos Hills, she quickly replied, "A haven—a hidden jewel. It's so close to see deer, wildlife, marshland, and yet you feel like you're so far away from the city because the vegetation is so lush."

SAG VALLEY FOREST PRESERVE

Some say this preserve's unpaved, winding trails provide more challenges than its northern sister, Palos Hills. This is the home course for the Palos Roadrunners and training ground for many South Side high schools. Try adding the 121 steps next to the toboggan slide to your workout, or take the alternate route and meet Big Bertha; she'll leave you winded.

ACCESS

Just 25 miles southwest of the Loop. By car, take I-90/I-94 south to I-55 (toward St. Louis), and exit at LaGrange Rd. South (Rte. #45, 12, 20). Parking is available at 119th St. (Forty Acre Woods), or take the Rte. 83 exit and park in the area at the base of the toboggan slide.

COURSE

Main route: For a 6.2-mile loop, head right under a viaduct to the other side of 96th Ave. You'll head left through Laughing Squaw Sloughs, and before the first mile you'll hit an uphill stretch—a prequel of things to come. After 104th Ave., for the next 2 miles you'll feel the challenge on your quads with plenty of small hills. At 2.5 miles, you'll need to hop over a little creek, and at 3 miles, you'll come upon a T-shaped intersection; keep right. This is by far the longest hill challenge, and at 3.2 miles, you get a bigger creek to navigate or slush through. From here it's downhill as you come toward the base and the toboggan slides at Swallow Cliff Winter Sports Area. Feeling energetic at this point? Go for it! Take a slight detour to charge up the 121 craggy, stone stairs to the left of the six enormous slides and come back down on the trail. Take the underpass back under 96th Ave. and turn right up a steep hill. Don't stop; go up and over, and soon enough you're back at the parking lot.

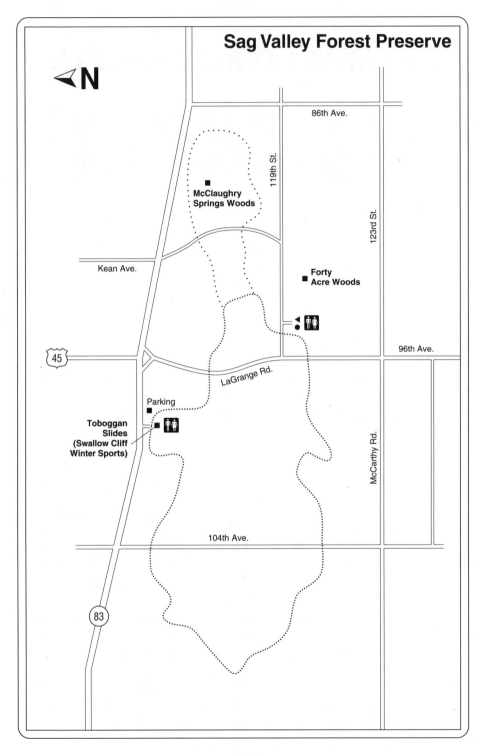

Sag Valley Forest Preserve

N

86th Ave.

119th St.

123rd St.

McClaughry
Springs Woods

Kean Ave.

Forty
Acre Woods

96th Ave.

45

LaGrange Rd.

Parking

Toboggan
Slides
(Swallow Cliff
Winter Sports)

McCarthy Rd.

104th Ave.

83

Alternate route: 8.7 miles. So you've heard about Big Bertha? Want to meet her? After you pass back under 96th Ave., keep going straight instead of turning right, and just when you think your legs can't take any more, you'll come upon McClaughry Springs Woods. Cross the bridge, and there you'll find, looming before you, one of the steepest hills on any trail in this guide: Big Bertha (so named by the Palos Roadrunners). It's steep enough to bring you to a walk, and Michelle Manzo-Slaviero, CARA's 1998 Runner of the Year who trains here regularly, warns, "It's a killer!" Tackle this regularly and you're bound to be ready for Boston or any cross country race.

TIP

Liam Flynn, the Palos Roadrunners coach, recommends treating yourself afterward at Lunes Pancake House at 124th and Harlem, where the Roadrunners often hang out after their Sunday morning runs.

SALT CREEK TRAIL
(BROOKFIELD ZOO)

6.6 MILES	PAVED TRAIL	SCENERY RATING					
		HILL RATING					

Lions and tigers and bears, oh my! They're nearby—at the Brookfield Zoo, of course. This is a delightful run despite a few major road crossings and lack of water; a favorite among western suburban runners and wheelchair athletes, too.

ACCESS

Approximately 30 miles southwest of the Loop. By car, take I-90/I-94 south to I-55 (toward St. Louis); two miles past the LaGrange exit, hop back onto the Tri-State Tollway 294 (15 cents), and within a half mile, exit right on Ogden Ave. (Rte. 34). You'll see a brown toboggan slide sign; the entrance is on the left. Don't turn into the first parking lot; keep going straight, and you'll see the trail entrance near the toboggan slides. Phone and restrooms are available here. If you want to start at the opposite end, by the zoo, take I-55 west to First Ave.

By bus, take RTA (312-836-7000) #304 or #331 or the special #333 Brookfield Zoo bus. By train, take the Burlington Metra (312-322-6777) from Union Station to the zoo stop at the Hollywood Station (four blocks south of the south gate). Contact the Brookfield Zoo at 708-485-0263, or visit **http://www.brookfield-zoo.mus.il.us/**.

COURSE

Perfect for a family outing! Check out this fairly flat, paved, 6.6-mile one-way path that winds through Western Springs, LaGrange Park, and Westchester and leads you to the northwestern entrance of the Brookfield Zoo. Street crossings are the only downfall, beginning with Wolf Rd. a half mile into the course. The next major crossings are at 2 miles (31st St.) and 3 miles (the busy 22nd St./Cermak Rd. and LaGrange Rd. intersection). The latter might be a good spot to turn

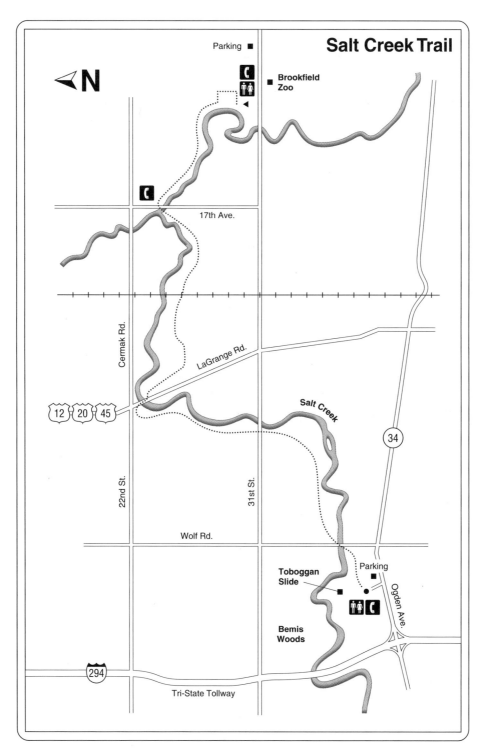

Salt Creek Trail

Parking ■

Brookfield
Zoo ■

N

17th Ave.

Cermak Rd.

LaGrange Rd.

12 20 45

Salt Creek

34

22nd St.

31st St.

Wolf Rd.

Toboggan
Slide

Parking

Bemis
Woods

Ogden Ave.

294

Tri-State Tollway

around, stash a water bottle, or make a dash into the nearby Jewel grocery store or Apple Tree Deli for some water.

The trail continues on the other side of the street, where you cross Salt Creek and head into a residential section. An outhouse is located at 3.8 miles on the north side. You'll come to a railroad underpass and shortly reach the 17th Ave. bridge. Protocol is important here; you'll be scolded if you don't adhere to the *one-way only* traffic policy. The Salt Creek Division Headquarters and a telephone are across this street. From here to the end is my favorite part of the trail; the forest is more dense and it leads you into the zoo woods (where an occasional breeze will alert your senses to the close proximity of animals). You'll know you've reached the end when you pass the British Home for Retired Men and Women and head into the forest preserve parking lot.

After you're done, a good way to cool down would be to walk through the 200-plus acres of Brookfield Zoo and check out the many attractions such as the Reptile House or Tropic World, a replica of a rain forest.

FOOT NOTES

The ever-popular Brookfield Zoo Run (5K) covers part of this trail; it starts in the zoo parking lot on 31st St. and continues onto the road at Maple St. For more information, call 708-485-0263, or visit the Web site at **http://www.brookfieldzoo.org**.

WATERFALL GLEN

9.4- MILE LOOP	TRAIL	SCENERY RATING	
		HILL RATING	

Not only is this one of the largest preserves in DuPage County but it's also the source of the limestone used to build Water Tower Place and the topsoil used to make Lincoln Park. This multipurpose trail surrounds Argonne National Laboratory.

ACCESS

Just 25 miles southwest of the Loop. By car, take I-90/I-94 south to I-55 (toward St. Louis) and continue to Cass Ave. South (#273A). Just a half mile off the exit ramp, turn right onto Northgate Rd. (the second entrance).

By public transportation: At Union Station, catch the Metra/ Burlington Northern to the Westmont station, and the RTA-PACE bus #715 will take you to the Argonne Information Center—but it will only drop you off and pick you up during rush hour, so you'd have to stay out there all day. Call RTA-PACE at 847-364-7223 to verify schedules.

COURSE

Although not as technical or challenging as Palos Hills, this 9.4-mile loop course offers an eight-foot-wide winding path that traverses through pine plantations, ravines, and marsh areas. The course also includes a few challenging hills and a creek crossing north of South Bluff Rd. For about a half mile at Westgate Rd., you will need to run along the shoulder of the road, which has light traffic except for employees coming and going from the Argonne National Laboratory.

The second half of the loop becomes more rugged as you follow the Santa Fe Railroad toward the waterfall area. At 5.3 miles, at Old Lincoln Park Nursery, you'll see a stone wall structure dated 1921. Be sure to follow brown trail signs (left), because there are a couple of confusing forks at this section. There are plenty of map boards that have helpful "you are here" notations.

Waterfall Glen

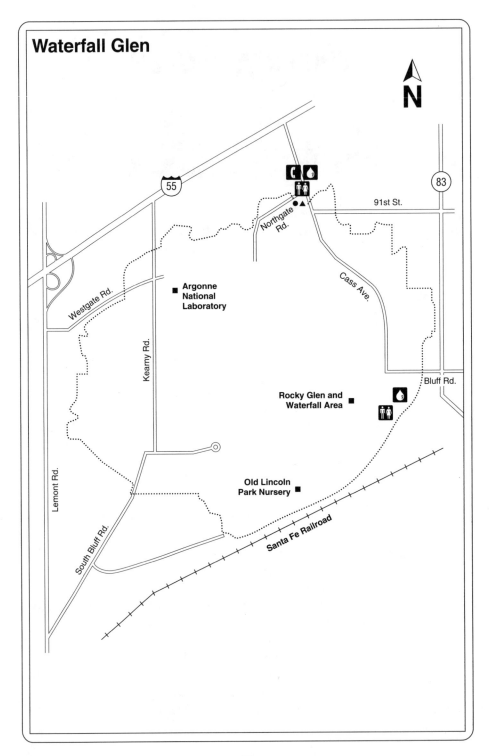

If you're lucky, as I was one cold fall day, you'll catch a glimpse of a snow-white fallow deer roaming through the woods; spooky, but mesmerizing. Although most preserves are a muddy mess after heavy rainfall, this trail dries out quickly. The carpet of pine needles in the fall will cushion your steps; in winter, tranquillity prevails on the unplowed trail.

Exercise caution at street crossings, especially at Cass Ave. (four lanes), which is at the end of the loop before you head back to the parking lot. The only restrooms and water are at the trailhead, so you'll want to carry water with you or drive ahead and stash some at one of the street crossings. For more information, contact the Forest Preserve of DuPage County at 630-790-4900, or visit their Web site at **http://www.dupageforest.com**.

TIPS

The Argonne Information Center (630-252-5562) is free and open to anyone interested in the laboratory's science, technology, and nature programs.

CHICAGO AREA ROAD RACES

Make no little plans. They have no magic to stir men's blood and probably themselves will not be realized. Make big plans. Aim high in hope and work. Remembering that a noble, logical diagram once recorded will not die.

—Daniel Burnham

1. Alden 5K
2. Arthur Andersen Bastille Day 5K
3. Chicago Distance Classic
4. Heart and Sole 10K
5. LaSalle Banks Chicago Marathon
6. LaSalle Banks Shamrock Shuffle
7. Marathon–Vertel's Turkey Trot 8K
8. Park Forest Scenic 10-Mile
9. Ridge Run 5K, 10K

This quote from our founding city planner reflects the same hard work and rise from the ashes spirit that have contributed to the success and longevity of these Chicago classics.

Although there are more than 400 races per year throughout the city and suburbs, these are some of the best organized and most popular. Some are massive: the 1999 LaSalle Banks Chicago Marathon had 24,621 finishers, a 43 percent increase from 1998. If you're looking for a reunion and party atmosphere, you won't want to miss the LaSalle Banks Shamrock Shuffle, Arthur Andersen Bastille Day 5K, or

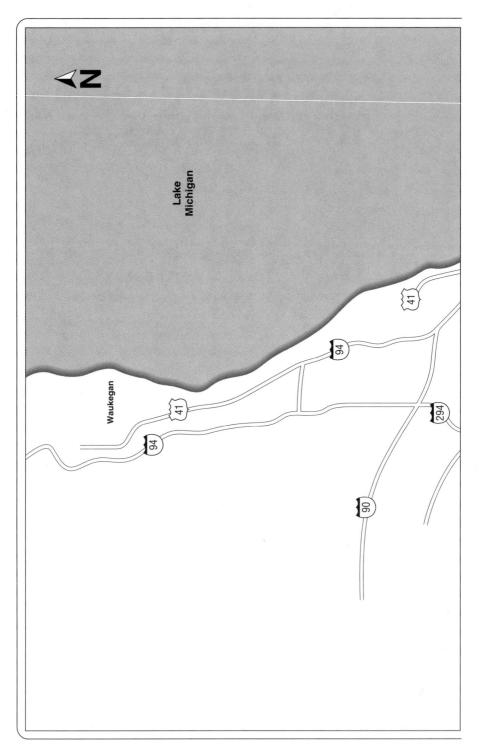

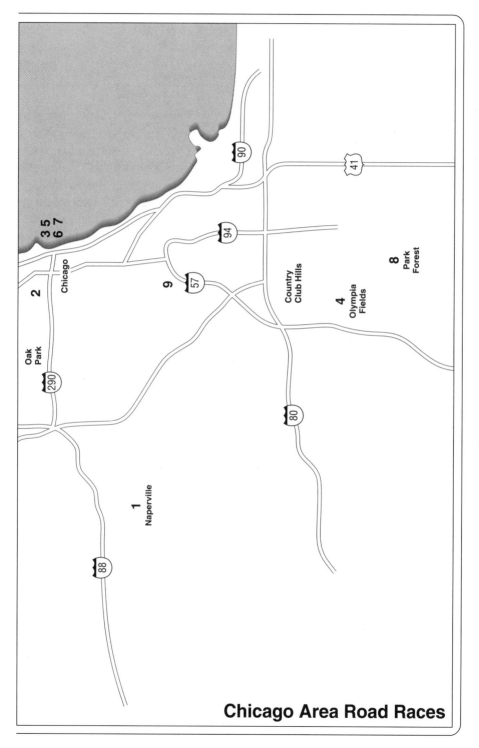

Chicago Area Road Races

Marathon–Vertel's Turkey Trot. Chicago Area Runners Association (CARA) members have awarded top honors to several. A few other races merit recognition. Each December, the Cross-Country Challenge at Indian Hills Farm (for information, call 773-878-3838) brings out the die-hard runners who aren't afraid to run through manure or snowstorms or to challenge high schoolers, who show up in busloads. Animal lovers and families won't want to miss the Bark in the Park (for information, call 312-644-8338) and Run for the Zoo races (for information, call 773-868-3010). One of the best debut races to date is Fleet Feet's Elvis Is Alive and Running 5K. Dig out your blue suede shoes, and call 312-587-3338 for information. I'm sure these races will inspire you in your running endeavors; they are an example of why Chicago is the city that works.

Two local sports publications offer race listings each month and have their own Web sites: *Chicago's Amateur Athlete* (includes CARA's official publication *Chicago Runner*) and *Windy City Sports* (see appendix, page 143). These free publications are available in most running specialty stores, health clubs, and local YMCAs.

CARA, with over 7,000 members, is the largest Midwest running organization. It offers a very popular Race Circuit, including a new Long Distance Series. As of this writing there are over 1,400 runners entered in the CARA LaSalle Banks Chicago Marathon Training Program, and beginners can learn from the Running Fundamentals class. CARA-approved races need to meet certain standards and are followed up with race evaluation forms. Located in the Loop, the association provides the running community with many valuable resources (see appendix, page 141).

Several city and suburban running clubs and specialty stores host fun runs, and there are a few organizations that offer track workouts. These are open to anyone; I highly encourage you to join these groups. See the listings in the appendix.

ALDEN 5K

5K	ROAD	SCENERY RATING					
	OCTOBER	HILL RATING					

Runners love to eat . . . runners love to eat . . . oh, did I mention that already? Event organizers are definitely in tune with our second-favorite pastime, since testimonials all mention the spectacular breakfast buffet offered after this race. Before you can enjoy your meal, however, you need to join some 600 others for this fast Naperville race, ranked #1 Best Short-Distance Race on the CARA Circuit in 1997, 1998, and 1999.

ACCESS

From the city, take I-290 or I-294 to I-88 (west). Take I-355 south to the 75th St. exit. Go west to Oxford Ln.

COURSE

This out-and-back course, shaped like a fishhook, starts south of the Alden Nursing Center on Oxford Ln. and heads straight down Oxford, which turns into Coach Dr. after Bailey Rd. Turn left just after the 1-mile mark to 87th St., then right on Plumtree Dr. and left on Cassin Rd., where you go down Rose Hill Ct. and make a sharp turn around the cul-de-sac island before heading back to the finish. I don't know what they put in Naperville's drinking water, but recent winners include local residents John Weigel, Dan Mayer, and Mary Knisely.

FOOT NOTES

This is a genuine "charity" event; all money raised goes to the Donald Davidson/Alan Brin Memorial Chapter of the Leukemia Research Foundation. The race started out as a fitness day, with a 5K race, Big Wheels competition (for toddlers), and tae kwon do and Jazzercise demonstrations. Eventually the sponsor, Alden-Naperville Rehabilitation & Health Care Center, kept just the road race, which has been extremely successful. According to race director Bill Wojcik, runners raised $140,000 in 1998. For more information, call 630-983-0300.

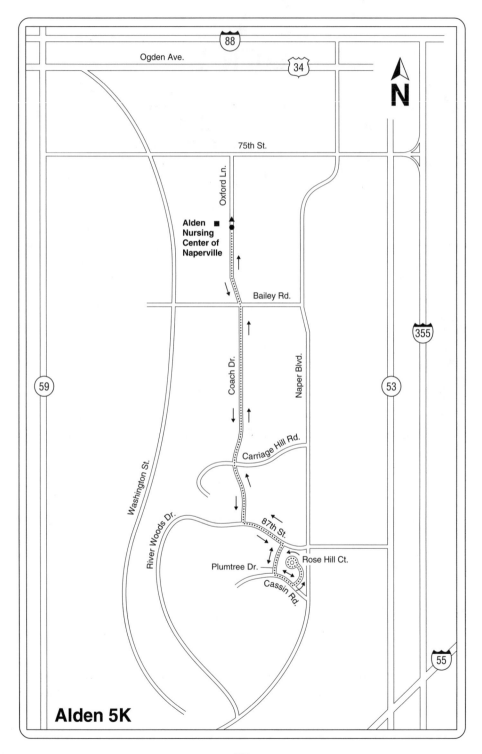

Alden 5K

ARTHUR ANDERSEN BASTILLE DAY 5K

5K	ROAD	SCENERY RATING					
	FRIDAY IN JULY	HILL RATING					

On July 14, 1789, the citizens of Paris started the French Revolution when they stormed La Bastille prison. This holiday symbolizes liberty and democracy much like our Fourth of July. It's only fitting to célèbre our sister city's holiday with Chicago's biggest block party for runners—a Friday night race guaranteed to close your work week with a hearty smile.

COURSE

Sizzle-sizzle, hot-hot best describes this midsummer race, which starts at the Aberdeen and Jackson intersection. More than 4,700 runners and walkers participated in 1999. If the weather warrants (and it's usually a pretty good bet it will), finishers are treated at the finish line area with cool water from rows of sprinklers. Everyone looks forward to the postrace party from 6 to 10:30 P.M., complete with live music, food, and an ample flow of beer and wine—all within the blocks bordered by Jackson, Morgan, Adams, and Sangamon. If you don't take home any prize money or an age-group award, try to snag the winning raffle prize—free airfare to Paris! The corporate team competition is popular, and proceeds benefit the Mayor's Office on Domestic Violence. This west-Loop venue draws some big names; course records belong to Khalid Khannouchi 1999 (13:38) and Jane Omoro 1993 (15:53). For more information, call 773-777-3261, or visit **http://www.arthurandersen.com/bastilledayrace**.

FOOT NOTES

Chicago's French Connection: When Daniel Burnham, our founding city planner, drew up the famous Plan for Chicago, the outline referred to making Chicago "Paris on the Lake." Throughout the years, our ties

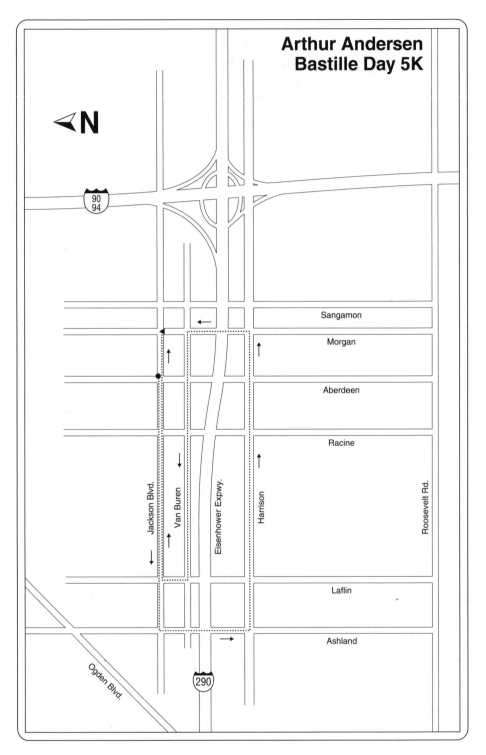

Arthur Andersen Bastille Day 5K

N

90 94

Sangamon

Morgan

Aberdeen

Racine

Jackson Blvd.

Van Buren

Eisenhower Expwy.

Harrison

Roosevelt Rd.

Laflin

Ashland

Ogden Blvd.

290

with France have continued. A 1996 sister cities agreement between Chicago and Paris prompted a local committee to foster relationships such as a runners exchange. In 1996, seven French runners crossed the Atlantic to run the LaSalle Banks Chicago Marathon, and in 1998 the number jumped to over 600. The marathon also has an alliance with the Paris Marathon and a scenic race in Lozere, France—the Marvejols-Mende half-marathon.

TIP

Hungry for some local French cuisine? Try Brasserie Jo (59 W. Hubbard St.), Bistrot Zinc (1131 N. State Pkwy.), or Le Bouchon (1958 N. Damon Ave.). Umm . . . you might want to shower first, though.

CHICAGO DISTANCE CLASSIC

5K, 20K	ROAD	SCENERY RATING	
	JULY	HILL RATING	

In 1976, *Rocky* won the Oscar for Best Picture, "Play That Funky Music" was a hit, and local race organizers thought a few hundred runners would show up for the inaugural Chicago Distance Classic. Imagine their surprise when a field of 4,000 swarmed the starting line. The oldest of all Chicago races has changed courses throughout the years, but it's still going strong.

ACCESS

By car, take Lake Shore Dr. to Jackson Blvd. to Halsted St. and turn left to Harrison. From the north, take I-90/I-94 to Jackson Blvd. (west) to Halsted St. and turn left to Harrison. From the south, take I-90/I-94 to Roosevelt Rd. (west) to Halsted St. and turn right to Harrison.

By CTA, take the Blue line to UIC-Halsted. By bus, take the #8 Halsted or #60 Blue Island on State St./Washington. For more information, call the CTA/RTA at 773-836-7000, or visit their Web site at **http://www.transitchicago.com**. Note: The American Lung Association of Metropolitan Chicago, which sponsors the race, highly recommends using public transportation to contribute to clean air—for healthy lungs.

COURSE

Despite course changes throughout the years (the lakefront to the west Loop to its new home base at the University of Illinois-Chicago campus), this race has managed to keep its unique length—Chicago's only 20K. The UIC campus is situated in the heart of two wonderful neighborhoods, Little Italy (Taylor St. off Halsted) and Greektown (along Halsted from Madison to Congress Pkwy.). The new out-and-back 1999 course will take runners from Jackson Blvd. to Wacker Dr., where they will be on upper and then lower Wacker Dr. This is not the most scenic area, but I can guarantee the shade will be welcome. From

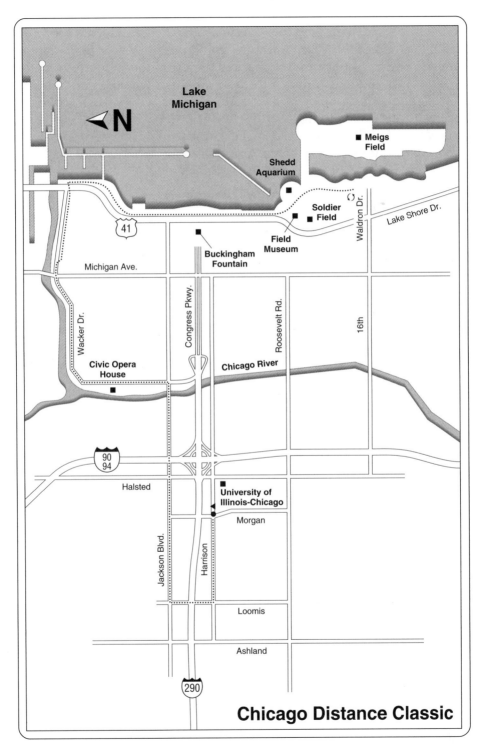

Lake Michigan

◀ **N**

■ **Meigs Field**

Shedd Aquarium

Soldier Field

Waldron Dr.

Lake Shore Dr.

41

Buckingham Fountain

Field Museum

Michigan Ave.

Congress Pkwy.

Roosevelt Rd.

16th

Wacker Dr.

Civic Opera House

Chicago River

90 94

Halsted

■ **University of Illinois-Chicago**

Morgan

Jackson Blvd.

Harrison

Loomis

Ashland

290

Chicago Distance Classic

here the course runs along the Riverwalk area to the lakefront running path via the new Museum Campus. You'll recognize two major landmarks: Shedd Aquarium (the world's largest indoor aquarium, with nearly 8,000 aquatic animals including beluga whales) and Soldier Field (home of da Bears and impervious fans who will sit through snowstorms—something to motivate you as you dig deep to finish the second half of the race). Waldron Dr. is the turnaround spot. Hot and humid conditions are a given for this event, rated one of the top 100 races in the country by *Runner's World*.

GO THE DISTANCE

CARA's 1999 Male Runner of the Year and Willowbrook resident Grzegorz "Greg" Olszowik won back-to-back titles in 1997 (1:04) and 1998 (1:05). His race advice: "Because of the time of year and weather you need to start conservatively; don't go all out. Keep yourself hydrated and use all the water stations." Originally from Poland, Olszowik also posted an impressive 2:21:24 at the 1998 LaSalle Banks Chicago Marathon.

HEART AND SOLE 10K

10K	ROAD	SCENERY RATING	[scenery icons]
	JULY	HILL RATING	[hill icons]

When running greats like Arturo Barrios, Mark Coogan, Ann Trason, and Grete Waitz (and even the late George Sheehan) tread these Olympia Fields streets, you know it's a classy event that draws these world-class athletes out to this south-suburban, midsummer, multi-award-winning race.

ACCESS

Approximately 40 minutes from the city. By car, take I-94 south to I-57 to Vollmer Rd. East. Go a half mile and turn right onto Crawford Ave. The race sponsor, Olympia Fields Osteopathic Medical Hospital, and registration area are three blocks down on the left.

From the Loop, take Metra Electric at Michigan Ave. (between S. Water and Randolph Sts.) to Olympia Fields at 203rd St. and Kedzie Ave.

COURSE

This winding USATF-certified race starts and finishes along 203rd St. (Burke Dr.). Granted, the course looks like a labyrinth, twisting through subdivisions, but don't worry about getting lost. Since 1981, the race's popularity has continued to grow, so be assured there'll be runners to follow; unless, of course, you're leading the way, aiming for one of the course records (Julius Mwangi's 1999 29:16 and Joan Benoit Samuelson's 1991 34:08).

FOOT NOTES

Voted Best Mid-Distance Race by CARA for 10 consecutive years. Why? Maybe it's the Sports Expo, with a variety of seminar topics such as "The Sermon From Mount Olympus: Great! You Won Your Race, It's Time to Vacuum." Maybe it's the opportunity to vote for your runner's premium (ah, to get a baseball cap instead of a t-shirt). Or it could be the theme water stops, where the Blue Man Group or a surfer dude might hand you a much-needed cup of water. Maybe . . . maybe you should check this out and decide for yourself! For information, call 708-747-SOLE (7653), or visit the Web site at **http://www.heartandsole.com**.

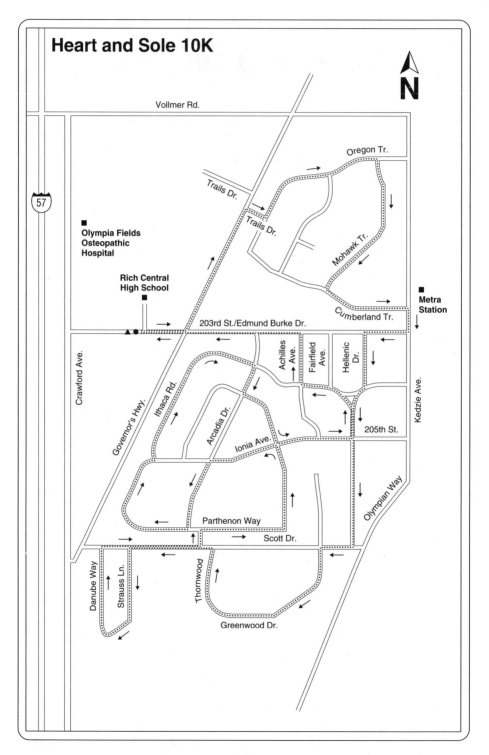

Heart and Sole 10K

N

I-57

Vollmer Rd.

Oregon Tr.

Trails Dr.

Trails Dr.

Mohawk Tr.

■ Olympia Fields
Osteopathic
Hospital

**Rich Central
High School**

■ Metra
Station

Cumberland Tr.

203rd St./Edmund Burke Dr.

Achilles Ave.

Fairfield Ave.

Hellenic Dr.

Crawford Ave.

Governor's Hwy.

Ithaca Rd.

Arcadia Dr.

Ionia Ave.

Kedzie Ave.

205th St.

Olympian Way

Parthenon Way

Scott Dr.

Danube Way

Strauss Ln.

Thornwood

Greenwood Dr.

LASALLE BANKS
CHICAGO MARATHON

26.2 MILES, 5K	ROAD	SCENERY RATING	
	SUNDAY IN OCTOBER	HILL RATING	

Success is marked by the journey, not the destination, and this race overflows with success stories, one reason it has been billed as "the people's race." How's the course? Let's just say this unique urban experience is fast, flat, and fun.

COURSE

After the Grant Park sendoff, you head north through scenic Lincoln Park to the ever-colorful Wrigleyville/Lakeview area (after Belmont Ave.), where you turn back south and cruise through Old Town, brush by River North, and head through the famous ethnic neighborhoods of Greektown, Little Italy, Pilsen, and Chinatown. You turn back north, just before the 24-mile marker, to the Grant Park finish beyond Roosevelt Rd. Last-minute course alterations do occur but are usually minimal. Weather can vary from sunshine and 50 degrees to 5 inches of snow (it happened in 1993). Remember, it's Chicago and anything goes, so follow the weather reports. Depending on conditions, you might need either sunscreen or polypro gloves.

HISTORY

Since its start in 1977, when the course wound back and forth through Lincoln Park and along the lakefront, this race has undergone numerous changes. Even the name has changed. It's been the Mayor Daley Marathon, America's Marathon/Chicago, and the Old Style Marathon/Chicago.

Dan Cloeter and Dorothy Doolittle were the inaugural winners in 1977, with times of 2:17:52 and 2:50:47, respectively. The first field of 4,200 entrants has since skyrocketed to over 29,256 entrants in 1999 (from 79 countries and all 50 states), and spectators numbered over 750,000.

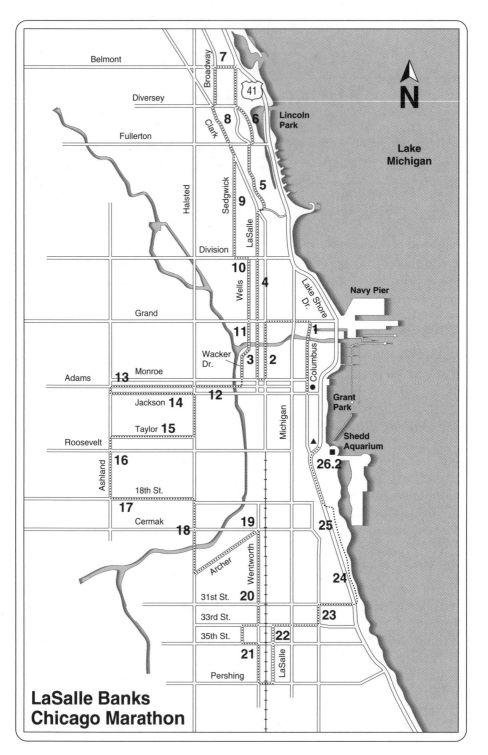

Belmont

Broadway

7

41

Diversey

Clark

8   **6**

Lincoln
Park

Fullerton

Sedgwick

Halsted

5

LaSalle

9

Division

Wells

10

4

Lake Shore
Dr.

Navy Pier

Grand

11

1

Wacker
Dr.

3   **2**

Columbus

Adams

Monroe

13

Michigan

Grant
Park

12

Jackson **14**

Taylor **15**

Shedd
Aquarium

Roosevelt

16

26.2

Ashland

18th St.

17

Cermak

18

19

25

Archer

Wentworth

24

31st St. **20**

33rd St.

23

35th St.

22

21

LaSalle

Pershing

Lake
Michigan

N

LaSalle Banks
Chicago Marathon

Kudos go to founder Lee Flaherty, of Flair Communications, who propelled the race from a dream to reality and kept it afloat during financially tough years. Other key players included members of the grassroots running community, who went on to form the Chicago Area Runners Association (CARA), and former Mayor Michael Bilandic, an avid runner. The race has weathered tough years, with fierce disputes over start times and controversial race director Bob Bright.

Carey Pinkowski has brought the race back from the brink of collapse (it was canceled in 1987) to the five-star event it is today. Pinkowski galvanized the fractured running community, partnering with CARA to start its highly successful marathon training programs. He's a savvy recruiter with a knack for spotting emerging talent. Under his leadership, 1999 prize money is at an all-time high—$709,800. Pinkowski, a Hammond, Indiana, standout and Villanova University All-American, even knows the course as a runner. In 1993, he captured his 2:20:19 marathon PR on these city streets. All told, he and his team at Chicago Events Management have brought this race to a higher level, which benefits runners of all abilities and is sure to continue into the next millennium. LaSalle Banks also deserves credit for its contribution of financial resources and volunteer support.

RECORDS

The mid-80s marked a pivotal time for women, when friendly rivals Joan Benoit Samuelson, Ingrid Kristiansen, and Rosa Mota propelled each other to faster times, culminating in Benoit Samuelson's long-standing American and event record, 2:21:21 (1985). After a decade of ups and downs, the women's contingent today is loaded with talented runners capable of challenging the record. In 1998, Joyce Chepchumba won in 2:23:57—a sure sign the women are closing in.

1997 signaled a new era for the men, when Steve Jones' 1985 record (2:07:13) was shattered by Khalid Khannouchi, 2:07:10, for the fastest debut and the North American marathon record. In 1998, Ondoro Osoro took Khannouchi's titles away with his 2:06:54 finish. But Khannouchi came back in 1999 with a dramatic surge through the McCormick Place tunnel (dubbed by Frank Shorter during the race telecast as "Pandora's tunnel"), pulling away from leader Moses Tanui to a sure victory clocking 2:05:42 and setting yet another world and course record. Chicago can surely claim that it hosts one of the most competitive races in the world.

For elite runners lamenting their advance to this distance, may I remind you that Steve Jones, Khalid Khannouchi, Ondoro Osoro, and

Marian Sutton all broke the tape with their Chicago debuts. Runners from outside the States have recently taken top honors (Greg Meyer was the last American male winner, 2:10:59 in 1982), but monetary incentives for Americans have attracted top-notch talent; for example, David Morris, who posted an American record for a loop course in 1999 (2:09:32). The following American women have been victorious in recent years: Kristy Johnson 2:31:34 (1994), Linda Somers 2:37:41 (1992), and Lisa Weidenbach 2:28:15 (1989).

FOOT NOTES

CARA and the race organizers have teamed up to offer an 18-week program tailored to all levels, and pace groups are available for those trying for either a 2:50 or 5-hour finish. You can even find marathon training advice on the Internet in Hal Higdon's LaSalle Banks Chicago Marathon Training Guide (**http://www.halhigdon.com/marathon/index.html**).

Prize money extends to the top 5K finishers, masters, wheelchair racers, and top Illinois finishers. Saturday morning's Breakfast Fun Run draws a good-sized crowd and is a chance to mingle with the elites. Water station honors have gone to the Frontrunners/Frontwalkers. You'll know why when you see them in the Wrigleyville/Lakeview area.

Whether you want to break records or conquer your first marathon, Chicago is your kind of town. Strong community support has propelled runners through this city of big shoulders. For information, call 312-243-0003 or 888-243-3344 (U.S. only), or visit the Web site at **http://www.chicagomarathon.com**.

TIPS

You want to enjoy the marathon but not run it? Gather your family and neighbors for excellent curbside action anywhere along the route, or ride your bike to Grant Park, run the Bally Total Fitness 5K, hop back onto your bike, and head west to catch the second half of the marathon. Prime viewing spots include Halsted (for the 12- to 15-mile stretch) and along 31st St. just after the 23-mile mark.

TIPS FROM SOME WHO OUGHT TO KNOW...

Here's some race strategy from folks who ought to know—past champions:

Joan Benoit Samuelson: "Don't let the distance intimidate you. Break the course down into a small number of sections and mentally click off each as you go by for a feeling of accomplishment. Also, take in all the people, sights, and sounds. If you focus entirely on your running, you'll miss out on a lot and won't enjoy the marathon as you should."

Khalid Khannouchi: "Run at a comfortable distance pace when you start. Make sure to not go too fast; get into a nice rhythm so you feel good, and then after the first half of the race, you'll be ready to pick up your speed."

Marian Sutton: "Listen to your body; don't overtrain; enjoy yourself; and take in the scenery."

Everyone has a favorite section:

Joan Benoit Samuelson: "It would probably be Greektown. When you get there, you know you're more than half-way home, and the sounds from all of the spectators' bells and whistles really give you a boost. The only problem with Greektown is that it smells so good you're tempted to stop and get something to eat!"

Khalid Khannouchi: "The last mile is definitely my favorite part. It's where I made my move in 1997 to win the race. Also, psychologically, when you hit the 25-mile mark, you tell yourself you're done! If you make it that far you know you can finish the race."

Marian Sutton: "I especially like the skyline at the finish; it's spectacular!"

LASALLE BANKS
SHAMROCK SHUFFLE

8K, 2-MILE WALK	ROAD	SCENERY RATING	
	END OF MARCH	HILL RATING	

Chicago offers numerous March traditions. Around the 17th you can peer over the Michigan Ave. bridge and watch as a motorboat putters below, dumping a canister of dye overboard, and presto! the Chicago River becomes an emerald-green waterway. Then there are the festive downtown and South Side parades, an opportunity no politician would miss. The LaSalle Banks Shamrock Shuffle is one tradition runners don't skip, and it appeals to everyone's Irish roots. Ranked one of the best races in the country by *Runner's World*, it officially kicks off the racing season and serves as an opportunity to gauge your post-winter fitness level.

ACCESS

By car, take Lake Shore Dr. to Monroe St. and walk south from parking, or exit at Museum Campus and walk north, or take I-290 directly into the Loop to Michigan Ave. Or take I-90/I-94 and follow signs for "Chicago Loop." Exit east on I-290 and follow to Michigan Ave. Parking is available on streets or in public lots (underground at Michigan Ave. and Van Buren, Michigan Ave. and Monroe, or Museum Campus).

By CTA, take the Red line to Jackson; the Brown, Green, or Orange lines to Adams/Wabash; or the Blue line to Jackson and go east to Columbus. By bus, take #146 or #6. For more information, contact the CTA/RTA at 312-836-7000, or visit their Web site at **http://www. transitchicago.com**.

COURSE

With more than 11,000 runners packed into Grant Park, the first left turn at Monroe St. can still be congested, and you're immediately hit

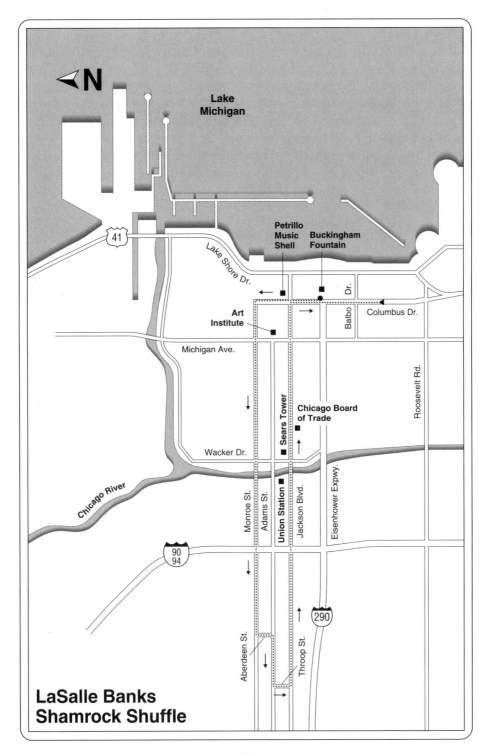

**LaSalle Banks
Shamrock Shuffle**

with an incline (no, it's not a hill!). You'll run by famous landmarks such as the Board of Trade. The short jaunt down Adams and Throop Sts. are the least scenic and the road condition is fair. Once you turn left onto Jackson it's 2.5 miles, sometimes windy, back toward the lakefront. More spectators line the streets around the 4-mile mark, and as you cross Michigan Ave. and go up that tough incline a leprechaun may whisper in your ear, "Come on, it's up AND over, don't let up!" At the finish line, a quick glance at the clock or your watch will provide the proof if your training has been lax throughout the winter months.

FOOT NOTES

Saturday night revelers will appreciate setting their alarm clocks later for the 9:30 A.M. start and will undoubtedly be first in line at the postrace party—complete with live music and refreshments. On a serious note, this USATF Indy Life Circuit stop (a circuit for masters, over 40, runners sponsored by Indianapolis Life Insurance Company) has become a masters magnet. In 1999, 12 masters ran world-class times. John Tuttle, 40, blazed to a 23:25 only to be outkicked by Olympian Todd Williams, 30, who set a course record of 23:20. This race definitely has a festive reunion atmosphere for all who spent their winters training indoors, and it's a competitive event not only for masters and elites, but for wheelchair, team, and Clydesdale athletes, too.

TIPS

If green bagels and green beer aren't your idea of an Irish meal, try an authentic corned beef and cabbage dinner at the Fireplace Inn (1448 N. Wells St.), or visit Carmichael's Steak House (1052 W. Monroe St.), which serves traditional Irish dishes including beef and Guinness Stew. For drinks, food, entertainment, and socializing, you'll enjoy Kitty O'Shea's in the Chicago Hilton and Towers (race headquarters) or the Irish Oak in Wrigleyville (3511 N. Clark St.).

MARATHON–
VERTEL'S TURKEY TROT 8K

8K WALK	ROAD/ CINDER PATH	SCENERY RATING		
	THANKSGIVING DAY	HILL RATING		

Each year on the last Thursday of November, families and friends gather around linen-laced tables and give thanks for their many blessings before devouring platefuls of turkey, garlic potatoes, breaded stuffing, creamed corn casserole . . . and pecan and pumpkin pie. Since 1978, many Chicago families start their holiday with this race, sponsored by one of Chicago's oldest running stores, Vertel's. Although you may be tempted to trot, the objective is to burn as many calories as possible for your postrace gobblefest!

ACCESS

Starts at 2500 N. Cannon Dr., north of Fullerton and south of Diversey (across from the Nature Museum). By car, take I-90/I-94 or Lake Shore Dr. to Fullerton or Belmont.

By CTA, take the Red line to Fullerton. By bus, catch the #74 Fullerton or #76 Diversey; the #146, #145 or #151 Sheridan/Lake Shore Dr.; or the #36 or #22 Clark St. and Broadway. For more information, call the CTA/RTA at 312-836-7000, or visit their Web site at **http://www. transitchicago.com**.

COURSE

This is another race that has endured the highs and lows of the running boom, undergone several course changes, and managed to improve with each challenge. The weather can be sunny and pleasant or overcast with snow flurries and a thin sheet of ice on the ground. The start/finish line is at Chicago's new state-of-the-art Nature Museum.

The first 1.5 miles on the street permit runners to thin out as you head past one of Chicago's treasures, the Lincoln Park Zoo (not only the

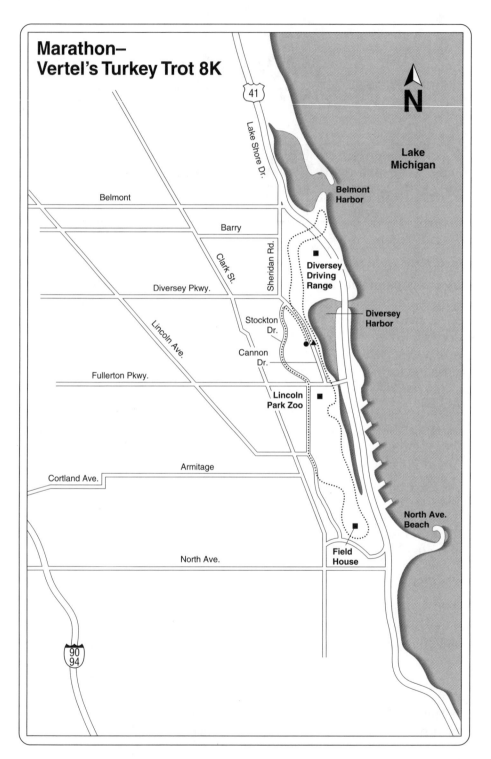

Marathon–
Vertel's Turkey Trot 8K

N

Lake Michigan

41

Lake Shore Dr.

Belmont

Barry

Clark St.

Sheridan Rd.

Belmont Harbor

Diversey Pkwy.

■
Diversey Driving Range

Diversey Harbor

Lincoln Ave.

Stockton Dr.

Cannon Dr.

●▲

Fullerton Pkwy.

Lincoln Park Zoo
■

Armitage

Cortland Ave.

North Ave. Beach

■
Field House

North Ave.

90
94

nation's oldest but also free). You'll cut over the bridge by the Farm-in-the-Zoo and Café Brauer and head down a small hill by the Grant statue (a popular meeting spot for runners). From here, you head south on the lakefront path around the Field House (2-mile mark) and then turn north to the Barry St. underpass (4-mile mark) for the turnaround. The last mile takes you past the Diversey Driving Range to the finish on Cannon Dr.

The atmosphere of this race can be described as fun with friendly competitiveness among extended family members, who may run regularly or only on this day, when they're visiting Chicago relatives. For more information, call 773-248-7400, or check out the Web site at **http://www.chicagoaa.com/turkeytrot**.

FOOT NOTES

Everyone is encouraged to bring canned goods to donate with their registration, benefiting the Greater Chicago Food Depository. According to store manager Will Bridge, over 5,500 pounds of food were donated in 1999; that's enough to provide 4,200 meals.

TIP

In 1857, the Chicago Academy of Sciences was established as Chicago's first museum devoted to Midwest ecology and natural history. The new Peggy Notebaert Nature Museum is host to many fun-filled exhibits such as the butterfly haven, which has a 28-foot tall greenhouse where butterflies can flutter about freely with visitors. For more information, call 773-755-5100 or check out the Web site at **http://www. chias.org/museum/index/html**.

PARK FOREST SCENIC 10-MILE

10 MILES, 5K	ROAD	SCENERY RATING				
	FIRST MONDAY IN SEPTEMBER	HILL RATING				

Labor Day honors the contributions workers have made to the prosperity and well-being of our country. Park Forest, one of the first post-WWII planned communities, celebrates this holiday by welcoming runners with open arms and a variety of music. You might even be cheered on by family reunion elders doing the wave from their curbside lawn chairs. Ranked one of the best races in the United States, it's a family affair in more ways than you'd expect. . . .

ACCESS

If you are driving from the city, take I-94 south to I-57; exit east on Rte. 30 (Lincoln Hwy.). Continue three miles east to N. Orchard Dr., turn right, and head 1.5 miles south, just past Lakewood Blvd., to the Plaza Shopping Center.

Or, from the Loop, take the Metra Electric at Michigan Ave. (between S. Water and Randolph Sts.) to the Richton Park I. C. station on Sauk Trail, east of Governor's Hwy. It's a 1.5-mile jogging distance from the starting line. For more information, call the CTA/RTA at 773-836-7000, or visit their Web site at **http://www.metrarail.com**.

COURSE

Start on Indianwood to Western Ave. to Chestnut, which leads into the forest preserve path for the next 4 miles. A musical sendoff and some surprise inclines will have your attention until approximately 4.5 miles, when you exit the shady reprieve, taking a right on Cromwell and then a left to Chestnut St. to the halfway mark before turning left down Western Ave. Turn right at Apple Ln. for the next mile to S. Orchard, which curves into Shabbona. Just after the eighth mile, it curves into Blackhawk Dr., where you make a U-turn onto Miami (9-mile alert— watch for the cheerleaders). From here, you head back to Indianwood

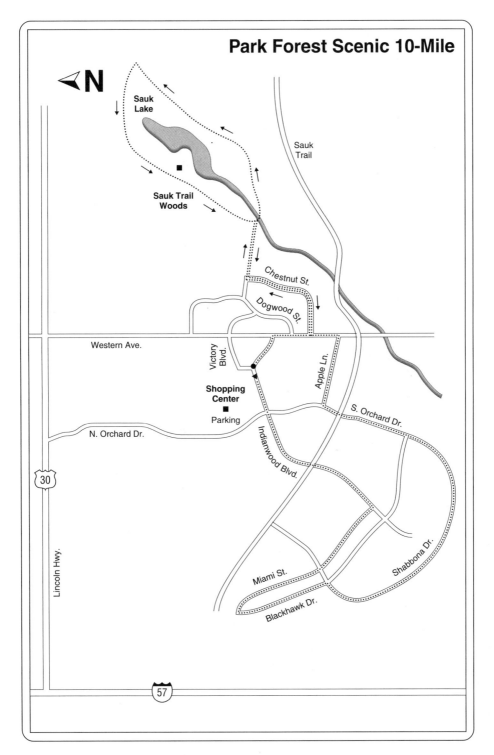

Park Forest Scenic 10-Mile

N

Sauk Lake

Sauk Trail

Sauk Trail Woods

Chestnut St.

Dogwood St.

Western Ave.

Victory Blvd.

Apple Ln.

Shopping Center

Parking

S. Orchard Dr.

N. Orchard Dr.

Indianwood Blvd.

30

Shabbona Dr.

Lincoln Hwy.

Miami St.

Blackhawk Dr.

57

Blvd. for your final mile, a fast straightaway stretch past some interesting music groups to the finish line.

FOOT NOTES

This slightly hilly route is one of the few permanently marked race courses, allowing for year round training. Mark this down: there is no race day registration; in fact, the cutoff date is usually a week prior to the race, and there's a 2,000 runner limit. For elite runners, the records to break are Jimmy Muindi's 1995 46:51 and Patty Murray's 1998 54:08. A chance at the money pot (over $20,000 offered) is one reason this race draws an extremely competitive field; other reasons are the USATF Women's National Championship and Illinois State Championship awards, as well as a unique award, suggested by a sponsor, to the most improved runner from the previous year. In addition to prerace training runs and a prerace day clinic, there's a 5K run, perfect for runners waiting for their friends or family to finish the longer distance. For more information, call 708-748-2005. E-mail: parks@parkforest.org. On the Web: **http://www.parkforest.org**.

You might want to hook up with the Park Forest Running and Pancake Club (see appendix). The club hosts several intriguing theme runs such as the Caribbean Cruise, a Fools Run, a Progressive Marathon, and a monthly Moon Run—where howling is allowed!

IT'S A FAMILY AFFAIR

This race is truly a family affair for the James and Utes families. Not only is Bud James the race director, but he's also the husband *and* coach of Cindy James, a Homewood native and one of Chicagoland's top distance runners. Cindy tied for third in the 1998 USARC series and is a four-time Olympic Trials Marathon qualifier with a 2:36 PR. Cindy's father is Warren Utes, a masters runner extraordinaire who holds numerous U.S. age-group records. Bud James explains that the family affair extends to all involved, including the Park Forest Running and Pancake Club. "Everyone involved takes pride in this race. Cindy is my right-hand person, and I call Warren my course director." Utes inspects the course regularly and informs his son-in-law of any pavement flaws or potholes that might interfere with this quality course.

RIDGE RUN 5K, 10K

| 5K, 10K | ROAD | SCENERY RATING | |
| | MEMORIAL DAY | HILL RATING | |

Question: What Chicago neighborhood is 30 to 40 feet higher than the rest of the city? Answer: Beverly/Morgan Park. This South Side community sits on a glacial ridge, and as a result, actually has a *real* hill—*within* city limits.

ACCESS

From the city, drive I-94 south and exit on 95th St. Continue approximately 3 miles (west) to Longwood Dr. By Metra, take the Rock Island District to 95th St. By CTA, take the Red line to the end, 95th St., and catch either the 95W or PACE #381 to Longwood Dr.

COURSE

A nice wide start on Longwood Dr., just south of 96th St. (next to Ridge Park), takes you gently downhill past several landmark houses offset by sprawling lawns lined with cheering spectators and music (patriotic to disco) blaring from stereos. The fun ends abruptly at 1.5 miles as you turn the corner at 111th to face a sharp uphill challenge. The rest of the course snakes through scenic streets with plenty of water stops. Just after you turn from Seeley to 107th, you get a downhill break before the long trip back up Longwood Dr., which seems to take forever because the slight curves keep the finish line from view for a tough last stretch.

The 5K course has the same start/finish on Longwood Dr., turns right on 108th to Seeley and right again onto 103rd, and left back on Longwood Dr. to the finish. With an hour between start times, you have the opportunity to do a double if you're feeling ambitious. Stick around afterward and enjoy Chicago's oldest Memorial Day parade. For more information, contact the Beverly Area Planning Association at 773-233-3100 or **http://www.bapa.org**.

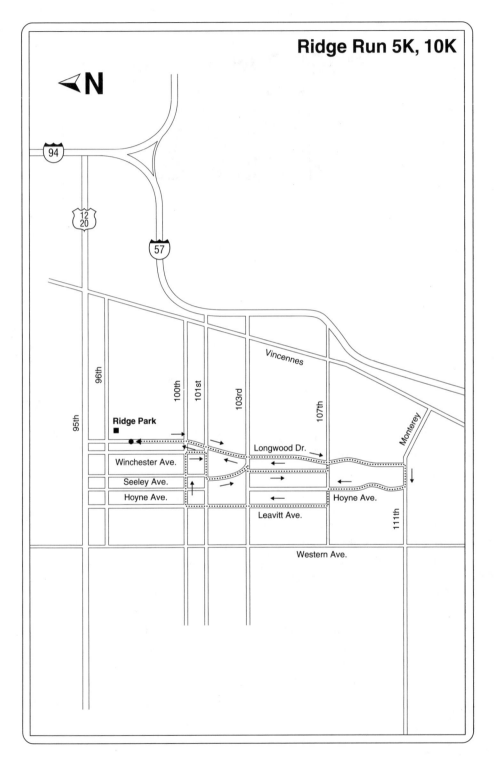

Ridge Run 5K, 10K

APPENDIX

The following information was correct at the time of publication.

CHICAGO AREA RUNNING CLUBS

Chicago Area Runners Association (CARA)
312-666-9836
http://www.cararuns.org

Alpine Runners (Lake Zurich)
Contact: Beth Onines, 847-438-8843
http://nsn.nslsilus.org/eakhome/alpine/index.html

Arlington Trotters (Arlington Heights)
Contact: Phil Richardson, 847-520-1866
http://www.geocities.com/HotSprings/4179

Evanston Running Club
Contact: Keith Holzmueller, 847-475-0630
http://www.nsn.org/evkhome/erc

Elmhurst Running Club
Contact: Susan and Darryl May, 630-941-0926

Foster Beach Running Club
Contact: Christine Knaus, 773-743-0661

Fox River Trail Runners (Geneva, Batavia, and St. Charles)
Contact: Gary Moss, 630-208-6677
http://www.frtr.org

Frontrunners/Frontwalkers Chicago (gay and lesbian club)
Contact: Jim Franzen, 312-529-4492; hotline 312-409-2790
http://www.webcom.com/bkm/ifr/clubs/chicago/

Hash House Harriers
Contact: hotlines, 312-409-BEER or 630-904-3915
http://home.att.net/~catboy-chi/CH3.html

Jim Spivey Running Club (Wheaton)
Contact: Jim Spivey, 773-702-4640

Lake Forest/Lake Bluff Running Club
Contact: Marty Rosenthal, 847-926-0237

Liberty Road and Track Club (Libertyville)
Contact: Maureen Snider, 847-362-2905, x5275

Lisle Windrunners
Contact: Bob Theodore, 630-585-4695

Lincoln Park Pacers
Contact: Michelle O'Brien, 773-528-6639 or hotline 312-409-3039
http://www.geocities.com/Colosseum/Track/7286/

Niles West/Oakton Runners Club
Contact: Patrick Savage, 847-568-3745

North Central College Track Club (Naperville)
Contact: Hal Carlson, 630-898-6772
http://www.cararuns.org/runningclubs/ncctc.html

Oak Park Runners Club
Contact: Paul Oppenheim, 708-848-3365
http://www.orik.com/oakpark.htm

Panteras Runners Club
Contact: Bernardo Gomez de la Casa, 312-320-9532

Park Forest Running and Pancake Club
Contact: Marietta Faso, 708-754-8102
http://www.lincolnnet.net/pfrpc/

Palos Roadrunners
Contact: Liam Flynn, 708-448-9200

Rainbow Road Runners
Contact: Charles Tucker, 773-324-5524

Run Chicago (Chicago, Lake Forest, and River Forest)
Contact: Greg Domantay, 708-386-4833

Southside Runners
Contact: Gale Stoffregen, 773-582-5728

Sunjoy Track Club (Wheaton)
Contact: Gordon Beckmann, 630-681-9084

Sunrunners (Barrington)
Contact: Ken Cowan, 847-304-8863

University of Chicago Track Club
Contact: John Corrigan, 847-866-1300, x1349

MEDIA

Chicago Runner (the official publication of the Chicago Area Runners Association) is a special insert in each issue of *Chicago's Amateur Athlete*.

Chicago's Amateur Athlete. Published 8 times per year. 847-675-0200; run@chicagoaa.com; http://www.chicagoaa.com

Windy City Sports. Published 12 times per year. 312-421-1551; http://www.activeusa.com/Illinois/

Both are distributed throughout the city in running shops and athletic clubs. They include articles, results, event listings, and Annual Event Guide.

RETAIL

(Most of these stores offer fun runs and have racing teams.)

Active Endeavors
773-281-8100 (Chicago)
847-869-7070 (Evanston)

Competitive Foot
708-246-5520 (Western Springs)
708-524-0030 (Oak Park)

Dick Pond Athletics
630-665-3316 (Carol Stream)
630-357-6884 (Lisle)
847-842-1753 (Barrington)

Fleet Feet Sports
312-587-3338 (Chicago)
http://www.fleetfeet.com/

Murphy's Fit
847-869-4101 (Evanston)

Runner's Edge
847-853-8531 (Wilmette)
http://www.tre.com/front.htm

Running for Kicks
708-448-9200 (Palos Heights)
http://www.heightsgroup.com/running4kicks.htm

Running Unlimited
847-991-9466 (Palatine)
http://www.runningunlimited.com

Universal Sole
773-868-0893 (Chicago)
http://www.universalsole.com

Vertel's
773-248-7400 (Chicago Lincoln Park)
312-683-9600 (Chicago South Loop)

ABOUT THE AUTHORS

Brenda Barrera is a freelance writer and a regular contributor to *Chicago's Amateur Athlete* magazine. She has also been published in *Windy City Sports*. An avid runner, Barrera has been a Chicago lakefront resident since 1985. She is a member of the Chicago Area Runners Association and has received numerous age-group awards in running and triathlon. She currently competes on the Universal Sole racing team. Barrera regularly reviews sports and recreation books for *Booklist* magazine and is a program assistant for the American Library Association.

Eliot Wineberg is the founder and publisher of *Chicago's Amateur Athlete* magazine, Chicago's local running and multisport magazine. He is also codirector of The Running Network, a distributor of major regional and specialized running magazines throughout the United States. Actively involved in Chicago's running community since 1987, he is an avid runner and triathlete. His favorite running spot is the lakefront path near the Museum Campus, where you can catch him running or cycling early mornings.

The best running routes of three more American cities

New York Running Guide provides complete information on 44 of the best routes throughout New York's five boroughs, Long Island, and New Jersey. The routes are runner-tested and approved for safety, scenery, and enjoyment. For each route in the book, you'll find a course description, a detailed map, directions to the starting point, and an icon key that shows route distance, scenery, terrain, hill ratings, and available facilities.

ISBN 0-88011-765-6 • 168 pages
$16.95 ($24.95 Canadian)

Experience the best of the Bay Area in your running shoes. This handy guide features 35 of the most scenic and challenging running routes and 10 of the top races—from 5Ks to marathons—in San Francisco and the surrounding area. For each route and race course, you'll find directions to the starting point, a detailed map, and lots of additional information to help you get the most out of your runs.

ISBN 0-88011-703-6 • 160 pages
$16.95 ($24.95 Canadian)

Washington D.C. Running Guide presents the 32 best running routes and six most popular races in the area. This book offers inside information to a wide variety of delightful runs throughout the district and surrounding locales. Inside you'll find detailed descriptions and maps for 38 of the city's top running routes and races including easy-to-read icons for each route showing distance, scenery, terrain, hill ratings, and available facilities.

ISBN 0-88011-726-5 • 136 pages
$16.95 ($24.95 Canadian)

HUMAN KINETICS
The Premier Publisher for Sports & Fitness
P.O. Box 5076, Champaign, IL 61825-5076
www.humankinetics.com

2335

12/99